▼ ▼ ▼

Getting Your Math Message Out to Parents

▼ ▼ ▼

Getting Your Math Message Out to Parents

A K–6 RESOURCE

Nancy Litton

Math Solutions Publications

Marilyn Burns Education Associates
150 Gate 5 Road, Suite 101
Sausalito, CA 94965

Library of Congress Cataloging-in-Publication Data

Litton, Nancy, 1947–
    Getting your math message out to parents : a K–6 resource / Nancy Litton
        p.   cm
    Includes bibliographical references.
    ISBN 0-941355-20-9 (pbk.)
    1. Mathematics—Study and teaching (Elementary)
    2. Parent-teacher relationships.   I. Title.
    QA135.5.L55   1998
    372.7'044—dc21   98-18969
                                                                        CIP

Editor: Toby Gordon
Copy editor: Alan Huisman

Production: Alan Huisman
Book design and illustrations: Joni Doherty
Cover design: Jenny Greenleaf

Composition: Cape Cod Compositors, Inc.

Printed in the United States of America
05 04 03 02 01 00 99 98   1 2 3 4 5 6 7 8 9 10

▼ ▼ ▼

For Gwyneth,
who taught me
the importance
of attending to
each individual

▾ ▾ ▾

Contents

Introduction *1*

Chapter 1   Newsletters 5
Chapter 2   Back-to-School Night 35
Chapter 3   Parent Conferences 49
Chapter 4   Homework 91
Chapter 5   Classroom Volunteers 111
Chapter 6   Family Math Night 121

Conclusion *133*

Resources for Communicating With Parents
    About Math *137*

Introduction

If you walk into my second-grade classroom during the morning math period, you won't see children silently filling in answers on workbook pages or taking timed tests on addition facts. Instead, you might listen in on a lively debate about all the different ways a yellow pattern block can be covered using other pattern blocks. Or you might hear the children discussing how many more baseball cards Emily has in her collection after a month of trading if she started out with 32 cards and now has 43. You'll find students sharing their solutions and strategies, talking confidently about their ideas, and listening thoughtfully to one another.

There won't be pages of worksheets to take home and put on the refrigerator, but there will be plenty of mathematical discussion and learning going on. I measure my students' progress by their growing ability to share thinking that is clearly presented and increasingly efficient. Ideally, my students have come to trust that mistakes are learning opportunities; they're willing to take a risk even if they're not certain about an answer. When they become aware of an error in their thinking, they're able to take in that information and use it to deepen their understanding.

This approach to math education, which is evident in many other classrooms throughout this country, is different from the one that most parents experienced as young learners. And because of the differences, parents sometimes have questions about what they see and don't see happening in the classroom, questions that can make a teacher feel uncomfortable. I frequently hear—and have been known to join in—a rousing chorus of "Wouldn't it be lovely if we could just teach our students and not have to deal with their parents?!"

When I start singing this tune, it helps if I remember that when parents express concern they are also indicating that they are aware of their responsibility for their children's well-being. It's their job to make sure their children acquire the skills they will need in order to succeed in school and in life.

Sometimes the dissatisfaction a parent expresses with my classroom may actually stem from a fundamental lack of connection between the parent and the child. This is tough territory to navigate and is almost certainly beyond my scope. In that case my best course of action is to suggest the services of professionals who can help bridge the gap.

But often parents are simply expressing the confusion they feel when they look at a pedagogical approach different from the one they encountered as students. Because the approach is unfamiliar, it may look inadequate. Parents who were successful at math when it was taught in the traditional way—that is, as something to be memorized—may have trouble understanding why anything needs to be changed. The feeling may be, *I learned through drill and practice, and what was good enough for me is good enough for my child.* Parents who were less successful with school math may be doubly concerned that their children not be hampered by poor math skills. They may insist that their children need to be pushed harder than they themselves were. They may be thinking, *I don't want my child to be put at risk by lack of math competency. I'm uneasy about my ability to help at home, so I have to make sure that the school demands lots of hard work even if it hurts.*

Both of these attitudes are understandable given the experiences of the people holding them. Yet, as a teacher who has had the opportunity to watch many students develop mathematical competency, I know these attitudes aren't necessarily going to lead to the kind of mathematical understanding and ability my students will need to be successful in the future.

The parent who felt successful at school math in a classroom that emphasized rote memorization is probably giving much more credit to the drill and practice than it deserves. I know from talking to young students who enter my first-grade classroom with efficient and abstract ways of dealing with numbers that their facility stems from having already developed mathematical models on their own. I first realized this when Denny, a kindergartner, explained to me that he had learned to add and subtract double-digit numbers in his head by paying attention to yardage gained and lost during the football games he watched on TV with his family. Denny would have been very successful in a traditional math program because he already had the underpinnings he needed to make sense of the drill and practice. One of my tasks, therefore, is to explain to parents how important it is that all children be given a chance to develop mathematical models as part of the process of developing efficient strategies for arithmetical competency. Parents of children like Denny need to know that their children are going to have opportunities to apply their understanding to many different problems in many different situations and become mathematically stronger in the process.

Parents who feel their own math ability is inadequate need to be helped to understand that their children are much more likely to thrive if they have an opportunity to understand mathematics, not just parrot it back by following rote procedures and expressing half-understood (and quickly forgotten) definitions. They need to learn that mathematics can be engaging, even fun.

My goal is to take a proactive approach, one that anticipates and avoids finger pointing based on misunderstanding and lack of information. This is a formidable task, one that can include writing newsletters to parents, discussing math at back-to-school night and during parent conferences, using homework as a link between home and school, and working with parent volunteers. This multifaceted approach grows from my own experience as a learner: I know that I develop a much clearer understanding of new ideas if I encounter them in many different guises.

This book is based on my own experiences as a primary teacher and also draws on ideas from many of my teaching colleagues throughout the elementary grades. It is not meant as a blueprint for communicating successfully with parents but does represent the musings and ideas of teachers who have experienced both the pleasure and benefits of working with parents and the occasional sting of feeling misunderstood.

When teachers forge successful partnerships with parents, students are the ultimate beneficiaries as everyone joins together in the sometimes confusing but ultimately exciting and satisfying task of making sense of mathematics.

▼ ▼ ▼

Chapter 1
Newsletters

September 10

Dear Room 5 Families,

We're off to a good start in mathematics. So far our emphasis has been on learning how to work cooperatively with a partner and how to use and care for the learning materials in our class. Developing these basics is a prelude to a year of learning how our number system works and having experiences in geometry, data collection, and measurement. As the children become familiar with and responsible for the materials, they are taking charge of their learning, paving the way for a year of investigating, communicating, and most of all understanding the world of mathematics.

For your child this will be a year of solving problems in order to become both a confident and a competent mathematics learner. My approach is to provide experiences for my students that allow them to develop meaningful understanding—meaningful because it grows out of opportunities to think, reason, and discuss their discoveries and conjectures.

You can help by talking with your child about mathematics and being curious and excited about the mathematical ideas we are exploring in class. You'll be learning more about our mathematics program at back-to-school night, in subsequent newsletters, at our parent-teacher conferences, and through homework assignments. Feel free to come to class to see what we're doing. We're having a good time and getting started on a great year of thinking mathematically.

Sincerely,

Nancy

When I send out this beginning-of-the-year newsletter, I have several goals in mind. I want parents to get a beginning understanding of the breadth of what we'll be doing in mathematics; I want to discuss briefly how the children will be learning mathematically; and most of all I want to set an upbeat tone for the year. Rather than talk about the failures of past mathematics programs, I concentrate on the terrific year we have ahead of us as a class. By keeping this introduction simple and positive, I set a tone that says, *Your child is going to have a good year in mathematics; please support our efforts.*

Newsletters are my favorite way to communicate with parents, because they don't have to be hurried through. I decide when to send one home (usually every few weeks), so I can generally take the time to think through exactly what I want to say. Parents can read what I've written at their leisure, digesting the information as they need it. And I've discovered that newsletters do more than inform parents about the mathematics curriculum—they sharpen my own thinking about teaching and learning.

Whenever I write a newsletter, I have a good idea of what I want to say before I begin. I've usually identified a purpose. Often I want to give parents information that will help them understand the current work we're doing in mathematics. Sometimes I'm responding to questions or concerns parents have expressed to me in person. But there's always that element of going deeper into my thinking as I research and compose the letter. When I finish shaping my ideas on paper, I usually have a better understanding of the subject at hand than when I began. I'm much better prepared to explain my thinking clearly to others. By becoming clearer in my own mind about some aspect of the mathematics program, I'm better prepared to meet the needs of the parent community as well.

I've identified three basic types of newsletters. The one I use most frequently tells parents what we'll be doing in class; the second attempts to make it clearer why we're doing what we're doing; the third describes how the math program actually plays out in the classroom.

Explaining What We're Doing

When I begin a unit of study, I like to inform my parent community about it with a newsletter. The newsletter lets parents know what the class will be doing, prepares them for homework assignments that will be made during the course of the unit, and familiarizes them with the mathematical thinking in which their child will engage. I often use as a model the suggested parent newsletter included in the curriculum materials I am using. Here's an example of one I sent home based on a suggested letter to parents in *Place Value Grades 1–2* (Math Solutions Publications, 1994), by Marilyn Burns, part of the Math By All Means series:

November 22

Dear Room 5 Families,

We have begun a new math unit that focuses on place value and estimation. Our place value system allows us to represent any number with just ten digits—0, 1, 2, 3, 4, 5, 6, 7, 8, and 9. Children need many experiences relating large quantities of objects to their numerical representations in order to learn how our place value system works. For that reason many of our beginning activities will involve counting and estimating large groups of real objects (popcorn, lentils, tiles, stars the children draw, etc.). We'll count and recount the same group of objects by 1s, 2s, 5s, 10s, etc., to help the children develop their understanding of counting and quantity.

Children must also learn that symbols have different values, depending on their positions within numbers, and what those values are. The difference between the value of the 3s in 36 and 63, although obvious to adults, is not always obvious to children. We'll be examining number patterns on a 0–99 chart and also relating our number system to money. (Today the children learned a game in which they used pennies and dimes to make a dollar, keeping track of their growing amounts in concrete form with coins and in symbolic form with numbers.)

We've also learned a guessing game that requires the children to compare the size of numbers between 0 and 100. It's called Guess My Number and can be played at home with no special materials. Player 1 chooses a secret number from 0 through 99. Player 2 makes a guess. Player 1 responds with a clue, such as: "Your guess was greater than [or less than] my secret number." Play continues until player 2 figures out the number. (In class we've found out that this language can be challenging. What do we know about the secret number if player 2 guesses 48 and is told "Your guess in less than the secret number"?) In addition to providing number practice, this game also presents children with the opportunity to think logically.

Other activities in the unit will provide experience with ideas in the strands of measurement, geometry, and patterns.

From time to time, the children will be asked to teach someone at home one of the activities or games they have learned in class. These homework assignments will give you firsthand experience with the unit. In that regard, since Guess My Number can be played at home or in the car while you're traveling, I recommend that you play the game at least three times over the Thanksgiving weekend. One game consists of two rounds, with partners alternating between choosing a number and guessing the other person's number.

If you have any questions, please do not hesitate to send a note with your child and I'll get back to you as soon as possible.

Cordially,

Nancy

Almost all the mathematics curriculum materials being published today include similar kinds of newsletters for the teacher to duplicate and send home. In adapting the above newsletter from the published material, I rearranged the text a bit and made it personal to our class by telling specifically what we were doing. I rework suggested newsletters in order to:

1. Create a better match between the information in the newsletter and the audience. The authors of the published newsletters don't have the advantage of knowing the parents of my students. I delete any educational jargon parents might find confusing, and I give the letters a personal touch by explaining just what's happening in our class.

2. Give myself an opportunity to internalize the ideas conveyed in the letter. If I adapt the published newsletters to fit my needs, the language of the "experts" starts to become my language as well. And as I become more comfortable with the language, I understand what I'm doing more deeply and I feel more comfortable explaining what I'm doing to parents.

3. Help parents see that their child's schooling is in the hands of someone who is thoughtful; getting information directly from their child's teacher, rather than from a form letter, gives parents confidence about the experiences their child is having in school. I want parents to know that their children are engaged in a learning program that will support mathematical growth even though it looks different from the mathematics they themselves may have experienced in school.

Explaining Why We're Doing It

As teachers we need to understand the pedagogy that underlies the curricular choices we (or possibly our school districts) have made. When we truly understand *why* we're asking children to do a series of activities, we are able to do our best teaching. We know which questions to ask when a child gets stuck and are better prepared to make choices about when to stay with an activity and when to move on. We are also better prepared to communicate with parents: sometimes parents need to know not only *what's* happening, but also *why* their children are doing particular activities. When they have this kind of understanding, they're much more likely to support our program and be able to help their children at home.

So once or twice a year I send home a letter that goes beyond telling about the activities that we're doing and looks at the pedagogy that informs the curricular choices. Below is an example of a two-part series I sent home to the parents of my second graders.

March 19

Dear Room 5 Families,

This newsletter and the next one will give you an in-depth look at how your child is learning to add and subtract. I'd love to get your feedback during our upcoming parent-teacher conferences.

It's likely that the way your child is doing mathematics in school looks somewhat different from what you remember from your own elementary school days. Most of us learned to add and subtract using a particular algorithm (a rule or procedure for solving a problem). To add, we were taught to "carry," and to subtract we learned to "borrow." We did pages and pages of computation problems that were unrelated to any particular mathematical context. These assignments were designed primarily to help us remember the steps of the procedure we had been shown in class.

Because these methods are familiar to us, we tend to think of them as a standard for judging computational competency. Unfortunately, students frequently learn these algorithms without connecting them to the meaning of the numbers in a problem. And many adults who learned math this way are unable to figure out simple real-life problems. Algorithms were invented to streamline computation. They are useful tools, but because they allow us to bypass an understanding of place value, they are a place to end, not the place to begin.

The shortcoming inherent to our standard carrying and borrowing procedures as *teaching tools* is that they focus attention on the *individual digits* in the numbers rather than on the *quantities* that the numbers represent. Students who forget the steps of the procedure often make fairly outlandish errors without even realizing they've made a mistake. And even when they do follow the procedures accurately, students often don't understand why they got a correct answer. Here are some examples of common mistakes:

$$
\begin{array}{ccc}
 & & 49 \\
58 & 53 & \cancel{50} \\
+25 & -16 & -37 \\
\hline
713 & 43 & 12
\end{array}
$$

The good news is that there are many efficient ways to solve computation problems. In fact, second graders are very capable of constructing their own procedures. Suppose a problem calls for adding 58 and 25. Second graders often solve this type of problem by adding 50 + 20 to get 70, then adding 8 + 5 to get 13, and finally adding 70 + 13 to arrive at the correct answer of 83. This method is as efficient as the "carrying" algorithm because it is easy to keep track of, results in numbers that are easy to work with, and takes only moments to carry out. It is superior to the standard algorithm from a mathematical standpoint because the problem solver never loses sight of what the digits represent. And it can be used to solve any similar problem.

Most of us don't know that other cultures have historically used algorithms that are different from those currently taught in American schools. The following example, from an article by Randolph A. Philipp entitled "Multicultural Mathematics and Alternative Algorithms," published in the November 1996 issue of *Teaching Children Mathematics*, shows that some adults from other countries were taught the same procedure in their schools that many of our second graders devise:

An older man educated in Switzerland and a man schooled in Canada in the early 1970s both demonstrated that they had learned to add by starting from the left-most column. The man from Switzerland worked the following two problems:

$$
\begin{array}{rr}
59 & 481 \\
+16 & +926 \\
\hline
60 & 1300 \\
15 & 100 \\
\hline
75 & 7 \\
\hline
& 1407
\end{array}
$$

This algorithm is one that many elementary school children in the United States invent when encouraged to do their own thinking. That is, when asked to add multidigit numbers, most children will naturally begin adding the digits with the largest place value. This is quite natural for adults as well. For example, if two friends emptied their wallets to pool their money, would they first count the $20 bills or the $1 bills?

Of course, to solve the problem this way one has to know that a two-digit number is made up of a multiple of 10 and 1s and that numbers can be taken apart and recombined. These concepts are developed in class through games, opportunities to build mathematical models using manipulative materials, classroom discussions, and opportunities to solve many problems. When faced with the task of adding two double-digit numbers, the children use what they've learned about our number system to come up with a procedure that they understand in order to arrive at an accurate answer. Students have a profoundly deeper understanding of an approach they construct themselves *and* they make fewer errors.

Let me know if you have any questions about the ideas expressed so far. I'll continue my discussion next week.

Cheers,

Nancy

March 26

Dear Room 5 Families,

This newsletter continues my explanation of how children learn to add and subtract.

In the case of both addition and subtraction, it is not possible simply to tell children a procedure for doing a problem. Truly understanding what it means to combine two quantities to get a new quantity is a *mental* relationship that children have to make for themselves. The logical-mathematical knowledge needed to solve both addition and subtraction problems develops over time, out of many experiences. We need to respect and encourage children as they move through the natural stages of learning. That process can be uneven and is likely to include periods of confusion as well as learning. Children need an opportunity to form and re-form their thinking as part of the process of developing understanding.

Students typically go through several stages when learning to add and subtract. For example, some students might solve the problem 58 + 25 by starting at 58 and counting on 25 ones (59, 60, 61, 62, . . . 83). These students have developed an understanding of the concept of addition and their method does give an accurate answer. However, counting by 1s becomes difficult to manage and is likely to result in mistakes as the numbers get larger. Our goal for these students is to help them find more efficient methods of adding and subtracting. Over time they will learn to chunk numbers in an addition or subtraction problem so that the numbers are easier to work with. And students frequently can solve addition problems efficiently before they can solve subtraction problems efficiently.

The procedures that students develop in the primary grades can be applied to larger problems. When faced with a problem like 1462 + 1745 + 278, there really isn't any need to use the old carrying algorithm. Instead, one might approach the problem like this: 1000 + 1000 = 2000 and 400 + 700 + 200 = 1300; that brings the total so far to **3300** (jot that figure down to keep track of it); next combine 60 + 40 + 70 = 170, bringing the total up to **3470** (jot that number down); now it's a simple matter of adding 2 + 5 + 8 = 15, bringing the total up to **3485**. It hasn't even been particularly important to line the numbers up vertically. Only three figures have been jotted down in keeping track along the way. And most important, the problem solver can feel confident about the answer because the focus has always been on the quantities represented by the numbers, not the individual digits. Approaches like this one are efficient and accurate for solving virtually any problem. You might want to try making up some hypothetical problems yourself to get a feel for how this approach works.

In the past, too many children ended up disliking mathematics and believing that they were not good at it. We need to turn that perception around. Mathematics is all about making sense, so we need to teach it in such a way that the sense making is always apparent. If young children are given the opportunity to build a firm foundation of *understanding* in the realm of number, they learn that they can achieve mastery over an important part of our world.

Warmly,

Nancy

In writing these two letters, I drew on several outside sources to help me think through what I wanted to say. My goal was for parents to understand that a memorized algorithm is not the only reasonable way to solve a problem. I wanted them to get a feel for how children actually make sense out of performing operations that involve larger numbers. I wrote and rewrote the newsletters several times, asking colleagues to give me feedback before I sent them home.

The response to these newsletters was heartening. Several parents commented that now they understood what their children were doing when they performed calculations. During our spring conferences, some parents told me about the ingenious ways their kids were working with numbers. They remarked that now they understood how their child was able to perform mental calculations so quickly. Other parents mentioned that the newsletters really made sense to them because they themselves worked with numbers in the ways that were discussed. We were able to have an enthusiastic dialogue about the kind of mathematics the children were doing, a dialogue that showed an increased awareness of the learning process.

Writing a *why* newsletter is time-consuming and arduous, but when I'm finished I know I have something I can reuse in years to come. I also feel much clearer in my own mind about my teaching methodology, prepared to explain my methods to even the most ardent naysayer.

Describing the Life of the Classroom

A third type of newsletter, one that captures how mathematical activities play out for the children in class, can also be helpful to parents. A newsletter like this attempts to re-create for parents some of the life of the classroom as children go about the business of doing mathematics. My friend and colleague Suzy Ronfeldt, who teaches fifth grade, first encouraged me to try this kind of letter. I loved the idea because it offered a way to emphasize the positive attitudes that children develop when they're involved in a problem-solving mathematics program. Two of Suzy's newsletters, my favorites, are included in Appendix 1.1.

Another friend of mine, Jan DeLacy, coined the phrase "mathematical moment" to describe what happens when the bulb lights up and a student understands something for the first time or sees something in a new way. This type of newsletter is an attempt to share some of those mathematical moments with parents. Here's an example of what I mean:

February 25

Dear Room 5 Families,

I thought you might be interested in having a chance to hear about how the children are going about doing some of the activities I mentioned in my recent newsletter about our geometry unit.

As part of our study of geometry we've begun to look at fractional parts of rectangles. On Monday, the children were each asked to create a rectangle using 6 one-inch-square colored tiles. The instructions were to make half of the rectangle blue and half of it yellow. Here are some of their solutions:

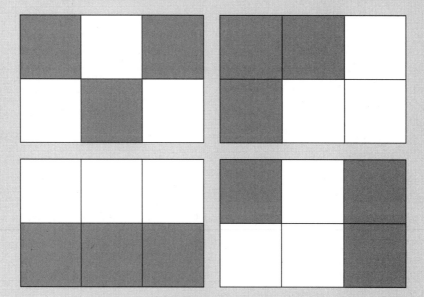

After looking at the many different ways the children had accomplished this task, I suggested they do the same thing using seven tiles. I was met with a chorus of, "That's impossible, seven is an odd number." I was delighted to see that the children so readily understood the flaw in my suggestion.

I then asked the class to investigate rectangles made up of 8 tiles, 9 tiles, and so forth up through 36 tiles, each time following the rule of making half of the rectangle one color and half another color. They were to explore which numbers of tiles were impossible. They were also asked to try to find a variety of ways to arrange the tiles for those numbers that were possible.

It was fascinating to see how much problem solving this activity brought about, especially when the children began investigating the larger numbers. There seemed to be widespread agreement that odd numbers were impossible, but no absolute certainty about which of the larger numbers were odd and which were even.

Tanya reasoned this way about the number 15. She explained that 15 includes the even number 10, plus 5 more. Since she knows that 5 is an odd number, she concluded that 15 was also an odd number. "You just take out the 10 from 15 and you're left with 5. That's how I know that 15 is impossible to make half and half." The look on Tanya's face when she described her thinking was priceless. She was full of confidence and delighted at her ability to think this one through.

I was delighted with Tanya's approach too. First, she was applying logical reasoning to figure out the answer for herself. That empowers her to figure out many more answers in the future. Second, she used her ability to decompose the number 15 into the component parts 10 and 5. This is a concept we've been working on all year in our study of number. It was great to see Tanya apply this understanding when solving a geometric problem.

For other children a checkerboard arrangement of two colors became a popular way of solving the problem. This method seemed to work well and it was easy to set up. Visually it gave the appearance of being correct. I asked Lana how she could prove to me that this method worked for any number. She decided to count the two colors of tiles that she had used for a checkerboard rectangle based on a 5-by-7 array (for a total of 35 tiles). She found that it was actually composed of 17 yellow tiles and 18 blue tiles. That sent her back to the drawing board to look for more accurate ways to determine whether her rectangles were half and half. What was impressive here is that Lana persevered in checking out her checkerboard theory. She was disappointed, but undaunted, when she discovered a hole in her thinking. She went on to try out many other ideas as she worked on the problem. She functioned as a mathematician working diligently and honestly on a significant problem.

This week's homework is an extension of our work with halves. Let me know if you have any questions or notice your child making any great discoveries when solving the homework problems!!

Cordially,

Nancy

A newsletter like this usually grows out of a situation that happens spontaneously in the classroom. To make sure that I capture some of these moments, I try to have a pad of paper close at hand on which I can jot down a few notes about the interaction. I try to think through not only what happened but also how I might describe the child's attitude and why I think the event is mathematically significant. Knowing that I want to be able to recapture some of these moments in writing encourages me to be a careful observer of what my students are actually doing every day.

Student work is also fodder for this type of newsletter. I like to pick out examples from a class set of papers that shows a variety of ways that children go about solving the same problem. This brings home the notion that there are many ways to solve a problem and that students benefit from having a chance to find the way that makes sense to them.

As I do more newsletters like this in the future, I'll keep track of which children get highlighted in each newsletter and make a point of finding ways to include everyone by the end of the year. I'll also make a real point of giving parents models of how to ask questions of children in ways that encourage them to think.

Using Today's Technology

When I was an English major in college I would start a writing assignment—an essay on a piece of literature I'd read, for example—by getting out a pad of yellow legal paper and a pen that felt comfortable in my hand. Frequently, I'd begin with almost no idea of what I was going to say. I'd jot down a few thoughts, reread what I had written, make some changes, and then say to myself, *Oh, yes, that's what I think.* I'd continue in this fashion, slowly building up an argument through the conversation that took place between the pen and paper and me. When computers first came along, I was sure they were not for me: it was the feel of the pen in my hand that got my thinking going.

Nowadays when I'm ready to write a newsletter, I first identify the type and purpose and then gather the background materials that will inform my thinking and writing. I begin the actual composing process by turning on my computer: I've put aside my legal pad and pen for the convenience and most of all the flexibility that today's technology offers. I make a point of jumping right in, getting my thoughts down as quickly as possible. The words I type first may end up in the middle of the letter later as I revise, making liberal use of the computer's cut-and-paste feature. I don't need to edit as I go, but can just charge ahead. But perhaps the best thing about using a computer is that I can reuse this same newsletter in years to come, sometimes with only minor changes. Knowing the file I'm saving can be used and reused makes the effort of writing a newsletter less onerous. And if new ideas have come my way when I'm next ready to use the newsletter, I can build on what I wrote previously, incorporating my current thinking as I once again make use of my favorite computer tool, cut and paste.

▼ ▼ ▼

APPENDIX 1.1
Examples of Fifth-Grade Newsletters

Suzy Ronfeldt's newsletters offer marvelous opportunities to her students' parents. Her detailed accounts of the mathematical life of her classroom reveal her mathematics curriculum and celebrate the thinking of the children. Suzy's newsletters frequently combine all three of the ideas I describe in this chapter and speak most eloquently when presented just as she wrote them.

November 26

Dear Parents,

The developers of the new TERC Investigations in Numbers units write: "Whole number computation is an area in which the elementary mathematics curriculum needs to be slowed down and deepened. Rather than being hurried into complex computation, students need time to develop strategies based on numerical reasoning. . . . When a primary goal is the development of sound understanding of the number system, students will spend much of their math time putting together and pulling apart different numbers as they explore the relationships among them" (Mokros et al., *Beyond Arithmetic*, 1995). In this letter, I try to explain what we are about in our numerical reasoning with whole numbers.

Division

1. *Making sense of the numbers by providing a context.* When I ask children, What is 100 divided by 7?, I want them to *think* of a context for the numbers in the real world—"There were 100 pennies in the jar and the pennies were to be shared fairly among 7 friends." This is a sharing problem and refers to how many in each group. Or, I want the children to *think of a context* for the numbers in a fictional world—"There were 100 aliens who wanted to fly to Earth from their planet, Ergo. Since only 7 aliens could fly on each space ship, how many space ships are needed for all 100 to make the journey?" This is a grouping problem and refers to how many groups.

2. *Making sense of the numbers using pictures or manipulatives.* One way children can make sense of these numbers is to *draw pictures* of jars and divvy up the pennies via their drawings. Another is to get out 100 beans (*manipulatives*) to equal the aliens and put out groups of 7 to see how many groups they will get. In both situations, the children need to deal with the remainders in a "reasonable" way. They cannot swallow the extra pennies or "eliminate" the extra aliens! The emphasis is on children's making sense of 100 divided by 7 in a context.

3. *Making sense of the numbers by reasoning mentally.* In addition, I want my students to approach 100 divided by 7 by thinking of what they know for sure mentally (without paper and pencil). I want them to think and reason about the magnitude of the numbers and the relationship of one number to another. For example, "I know for sure that 7 times 10 equals 70 ($7 \times 10 = 70$) so I know for certain that each child will get 10 pennies. Now I have to deal with the remaining 30 pennies. I know for sure that 7 children times 4 pennies each will use up 28 of the 30 pennies ($7 \times 4 = 28$). Therefore each child will get 14 (10 + 4) pennies altogether, and there will be 2 pennies left over. Now I understand that 7 times 14 equals 98 with 2 left over, so I realize that 100 divided by 7 equals 14 R 2." Here the child is *breaking problems into smaller, more familiar components.* She is thinking of 100 as 70 + 30. Another student might think of 100 as 50 + 50. Still another way to reason mentally would be to skip count by 7s until you get close to 100 and keep track of the number of counts (7, 14, 21, 28 . . . 98, with two more to get to 100). **Please look at the attached page showing how children made sense of 65 divided by 5 in a grouping context. There are a variety of strategies here.**

4. *Using the division notation.* As children use pictures or manipulatives and as they reason mentally, they are encouraged to use the proper division notation:

$$100 \div 7 = 14R2 \qquad\qquad 7\overline{)100}^{\,14R2}$$

5. *Using the division algorithm.* At this point I know some of you are thinking, *Why take all this time to get to this point, especially since you and I started and ended at this point when we were in school?* But how many of us really understood the magnitude of the numbers and the relationship of one number to another when we were doing the traditional algorithm in elementary school? I believe this was our thinking: 7 goes into 10 (is that really a 10 or is it 100?) once, so I put a 1 above the 10 (*divide*). Next I go 1 times 7 (*multiply*) and write 7 below the 10. Then I take 7 from 10 to get 3 (*subtract*). Finally I *bring down* the 0 to make 3 into 30. Next I think, 7 goes into 28 four times and follow the previous steps.

$$7\overline{)100} \quad \frac{14R2}{}$$
$$\underline{-7}$$
$$30$$
$$\underline{-28}$$
$$2$$

What happened when we forgot some or all of the steps involved? Were we able to make sense of the problem using other strategies? I can remember learning to recite Dad (*divide*), Mother (*multiply*), Sister (*subtract*), and Brother (*bring down*) in grade school. These words certainly had nothing to do with my understanding of the numbers. I was rotely following a procedure instead of "thinking mathematically."

Multiplication

The same five approaches mentioned above to making sense of numbers are relevant to what we are doing in multiplication. From the first week of school, we have used multiplication in a context as we write word problems. We have also used pictures or manipulatives such as rectangular arrays to build an understanding of factors and multiples, to "know" our basic facts.

Now we are making sense of our more difficult multiplication facts by *breaking the numbers into more familiar parts* (6×9 becomes $3 \times 9 + 3 \times 9$), by *approximating to more familiar numbers* (6×9 becomes 6×10 first, then subtract 6), and by *skip counting* (6, 12, 18 . . . 54, taking 9 counts. Yes, (5×10) + 4 does get the right answer of 54, but this approach does not lead to a better understanding of why $6 \times 9 = 54$. **The strategies on the attached page dealing with $6 \times 9 = 54$ do lead to a better understanding of the numbers.**

Also, **look at the attached page dealing with $38 \times 2 = 76$**. Notice how many of the children are thinking of 38 as 30 + 8, *breaking the number into familiar components*. Evan begins with 35 and Lisa with 40 because they feel these are *more familiar numbers* to deal with at first. I am surprised no one uses the halving idea here (since I know 19 is half of 38, I am going to multiply $19 \times 2 = 38$ and then double that answer to arrive at 76). It is used often in class.

In doing 38 × 2 vertically using the traditional algorithmic procedure, most children and most of us think this way: 2 times 8 is 16. Put down the 6 and carry the 1 above the 3. Next take 2 times 3, which equals 6 and add on the 1. By rotely following the procedure, we do get the correct answer, but do we have a deep understanding that we are really multiplying 2 times 38? If we forget the memorized procedure, can we think about and make sense of the problem using other strategies? To be mathematically powerful, we need to be able to do this.

Sincerely,

Suzy Ronfeldt

```
┌─────────────────────────────────────────────┐
│                    65 ÷ 5                     │
└─────────────────────────────────────────────┘
```

Pretend we have 65 students in our class and there are 5 people in a group. How many groups would there be? How do you know that?

Brad: I know that it is 13 groups and no leftovers because $5 \times 10 = 50$ and $5 \times 3 = 15$ so $5 \times 13 = 65$.

Kevin:

5	5	5	5	5	5
+5	+5	+5	+5	+5	+5
10	10	10	10	10	10 = 60 + 5 = 65

It takes 13 5s to equal 65, so there would be 13 teams.

Annette: $65 \div 5 = 13$ $\quad 5\overline{)65}^{13}$ I know this because I know $11 \times 5 = 55 + 10 = 65; 10 = 2 \times 5$.

Anna: What I knew first was that there were 10 5s in 50 because $5 \times 10 = 50$, so that's 10 5s, and $50 + 15 = 65$. There are 3 5s in 15 because $3 \times 5 = 15$. Ten 5s and 3 5s is 13 5s. There will be 13 teams. To check myself I skip counted 5, 10, 15, 20, 25, 30, 35, 40, 45, 50, 55, 60, 65.

Zander: I know $5 \times \underline{8} = 40$ and $5 \times \underline{5} = 25$, and $8 + 5 = 13$ so there are 13 teams.

Tessa:

Teams	1	2	3	4	5	6	7	8	9	10	11	12	13
Kids	5	5	5	5	5	5	5	5	5	5	5	5	5

I know there are 13 teams by skip counting by 5s.

James: I know $12 \times 5 = 60$, so then I know $13 \times 5 = 65$. This means there are 13 tables with 5 kids at each.

Davida: I know $12 \times 5 = 60$, so all I would have to do is add one more 5 giving me 13 tables $(12 \times 5) + 5 = 65$.

6 × 9 = 54

Your friend is having difficulty understanding this multiplication fact. How might your friend think about or make sense of this problem?

Ethan: Remember $6 \times 10 = 60$, then subtract one 6, and you get 54.

David: Think of half of $6 = 3$, then go $(3 \times 9) \times 2$, which is 27×2 and equals 54.

Lorena: $6 \times 8 = 48 + 6 = 54$. I know 6×8 is 48, but I need one more 6 to have 6×9, so I add $48 + 6$.

Josh: I know that you can make 9 out of three 3s. So I multiply 6×3, which is 18. Then, since 3 is $\frac{1}{3}$ of 9, I multiply $18 \times 3 = 30 + 24 = 54$.

Penny: I would do 5×9, because it is easier for me. $5 \times 9 = 45$. Then I would add 9, $45 + 9 = 54$. When you add 9 it is like counting by 9: 9, 18, 27, 36, 45 (5×9), 54 (6×9).

Victor: My friend could split 6 into two parts and take each part times 9: $3 \times 9 = 27$; $3 \times 9 = 27$; $27 + 27 = 54$.

Martin: (1) You could think of it as $6 \times 10 = 60$, then $- 6$ to get 54. (2) You could think of it as 5×9 and count by 5s (5, 10, 15, 20, 25, 30, 35, 40, 45) and add 9. (3) You can do $3 \times 9 + 3 \times 9$ and you would get $27 + 27 = 54$.

Elena: One way you could do 6×9 is by doing $5 \times 9 + 9 = 54$. Another way you could do 6×9 is by doing $(3 \times 9) \times 2 = 54$.

Matt: Pretend that the 9s are 10s $(6 \times 10 = 60)$, then take away 6 $(60 - 6 = 54)$. This works on other $\times 9$ problems too.

$$\boxed{38 \times 2 = 76}$$

Pretend you have a friend who is having difficulty making sense of 2×38 in his head. How might your friend think about or make sense of this problem?

Lisa: Two times 40 is easier than two times 38. 2×40 is 80. Then you $- 4$, because $2 \times 2 = 4$ and you can't forget the 2 $(40 - 2 = 38)$; $(2 \times 40) - 4 = 80 - 4 = 76$.

Evan: I know that you can think of 38 as 35, then take $35 \times 2 = 70$. But you have to remember the 3 and take it $\times 2$: $3 \times 2 = 6$ and $70 + 6 = 76$.

Mary: Think of 38 as $30 + 8$. Double both 30 (60) and 8 (16). Then add 16 to 60 to get 76.

$$
\begin{array}{ll}
30 + 30 = 60 & \quad (2 \times 30) + (2 \times 8) = 76 \\
\underline{8 + 8 = 16} & \\
76 &
\end{array}
$$

Jess: You can think of 38 as 30 and 8. You still have the $\times 2$ so you do $8 \times 2 = 16$. Then you do $30 \times 2 = 60$. Finally you add $16 + 60 = 76$.

Terry: Another way to understand 2×38 is to break 38 into 30 and 8; $2 \times 30 = 60$; $2 \times 8 = 16$; $60 + 16 = 76$.

$$
\begin{array}{cc}
30 & \quad 8 \\
\underline{\times\,2} & \quad \underline{\times\,2} \\
60 & \quad 16
\end{array}
$$

$$
\begin{array}{r}
60 \\
+\,\underline{16} \\
76
\end{array}
$$

Hasan: He might take away 8 from 38 and multiply 30×2, then multiply 2×8: $(30 \times 2) + (8 \times 2) = 60 + 16 = 76$

March 21

Dear Parents,

Your child had many opportunities to add, subtract, multiply, and divide with whole numbers and fractions as s/he did measuring and scaling problems dealing with Brobdingnag and Lilliput. You will get a packet of this work at our conference next week.

Often as we are problem solving and talking math (which happens daily around homework and class work), some child has a mathematical moment that we celebrate, because the "aha" enriches our own thinking and reasoning. For example, Kevin excitedly said, "I know $\frac{1}{4}$ of 12 inches equals 3 inches, therefore I know $\frac{1}{8}$ of 12 inches, because $\frac{1}{8}$ is half of $\frac{1}{4}$, so half of 3 inches would be $1\frac{1}{2}$ inches and that is $\frac{1}{8}$ of 12 inches. Penny, who was standing nearby, added with great enthusiasm, "Well, if $\frac{1}{8}$ of 12 inches is $1\frac{1}{2}$ inches, then I know $\frac{1}{16}$ of 12 inches is $\frac{3}{4}$ inch, because $\frac{3}{4}$ is one half of $1\frac{1}{2}$." A few days later Josh joined in the pattern of these "aha's" when he shared, "I know that $\frac{1}{24}$ of 18 inches is $\frac{3}{4}$ of an inch. I know this because $\frac{1}{6}$ of 18 inches is 3 inches and $\frac{1}{12}$ is half the size of $\frac{1}{6}$ and that would be $1\frac{1}{2}$ inches and $\frac{1}{24}$ would be half of $\frac{1}{12}$ and that would be $\frac{3}{4}$ inch."

These are the connections children use to make sense of mathematics instead of rotely following a procedure ($\frac{1}{24} \times \frac{18}{1} = \frac{18}{24}$, then divide 18 by 6 and 24 by 6 to reduce the fraction to $\frac{3}{4}$). When Kevin talked of $\frac{1}{4}$ of 12 inches, he was multiplying $\frac{1}{4} \times 12 = 3$ and he "understood" this from having used the ruler in the context of a real problem instead of rotely following a procedure ($\frac{1}{4} \times \frac{12}{1} = \frac{12}{4} = 3$). The children were frequently multiplying a fraction times a whole number in the context of solving real measurement problems in this unit.

When the children worked with partners to figure out mathematically the Brob size of an Ourland object and then actually measure to make this object, one mathematical "aha" was the idea that when you take 12 times the length and 12 times the width to make a Brob-sized object like a box of Nerds or a box of Crayolas, the area of that Brob-sized object is 144 times the area of the Ourland object! Be sure you look at the large objects and read the mathematical thinking involved in this investigation.

Right now, we are having many experiences at the concrete or the conceptual level as we grapple with the almost too many big ideas associated with making sense of fractions. (Rest assured, we will be returning to making sense of whole numbers after spring break.)

▲ Fractions can describe parts of one thing (fraction kit rectangle, 10-by-10 grid, pizza) or parts of a group of things (groups of people, M&M's).

▲ A fraction represents different-sized parts if the wholes the fractions come from are different sizes. (We haven't done many problems related to this idea yet.)

▲ Fractional parts are equal parts of a whole. Fifth graders may try to convince younger siblings that their half of a candy bar needs to be larger, but that is not fair shares, that is not fractionally correct.

▲ Different fractions can express the same relationship. As they make and use their fraction kits, the children begin to "see and feel" that $\frac{1}{2}$, $\frac{4}{8}$, $\frac{6}{12}$, and 50% all represent the same relationship. Tess had a mathematical moment when she wrote the following fraction kit statement for homework: "$\frac{1}{4}$ is greater than $\frac{1}{5}$. I know this because $\frac{1}{4}$ = 25% and $\frac{1}{5}$ = 20% and 25% is a greater amount than 20%." Percents certainly helped her understand the value of the fractions.

▲ Fraction number sense calls for being mentally able to estimate, compare, and combine common fractions. Ethan used fraction number sense on Monday when he said, "If we are to share 4 cookies with 6 people, I know right away that there are more people than cookies so everyone will have less than 1 whole cookie." Lisa and Brad also used number sense when they talked about the homework problem that asked the children to divide an 18-inch paper strip into 6 equal parts and to explain how many inches each part would be. They both said, "If $\frac{1}{3}$ of 18 inches = 6 inches, then we know $\frac{1}{6}$ of 18 inches = 3 inches, because $\frac{1}{6}$ is half of $\frac{1}{3}$, so 3 inches has to be half of 6 inches."

▲ In a fractional numeral, the denominator tells the number of equal parts the whole is divided into and the numerator tells the number of parts we're talking about.

▲ When the size of the whole changes, the name of the same-sized fractional part changes. (We haven't had many problems dealing with this idea yet.)

▲ Common denominators are helpful for adding or subtracting fractions with unlike denominators. One recent homework problem said that Michael ate $\frac{1}{2}$ of an orange, Hiroko ate $\frac{1}{4}$ of an orange, and Roberto ate $\frac{3}{8}$ of an orange. The first question was, *Who ate the most?* and the second question was, *How many oranges did they eat altogether?* To this latter question Joni said, "$\frac{1}{2} = \frac{4}{8}$ and $\frac{1}{4} = \frac{2}{8}$, so $\frac{4}{8} + \frac{2}{8} + \frac{3}{8} = \frac{9}{8}$ and that is the same as $1\frac{1}{8}$ orange." Davida added, "Well you could say $\frac{1}{2} = \frac{2}{4}$ and $\frac{1}{4} = \frac{1}{4}$ and $\frac{3}{8} = \frac{1}{4} + \frac{1}{8}$, so $\frac{2}{4} + \frac{1}{4} + \frac{1}{4} = 1$ whole orange plus that extra $\frac{1}{8}$ orange." Brooke joined in and said, "I prefer thinking of percents and I know $\frac{1}{2} = 50\%$ and $\frac{1}{4} = 25\%$. Then $\frac{3}{8}$ is the same as $\frac{1}{4}$, or 25%, plus $\frac{1}{8}$, or $12\frac{1}{2}\%$. I know $\frac{1}{8}$ is half of $\frac{1}{4}$, so half of 25% is $12\frac{1}{2}\%$. So you need 100%, which equals one whole orange, plus $12\frac{1}{2}\%$ of another orange."

▲ Fractions are intimately related to division. If you look at the next two pages, you will see the variety of strategies children use to make fractional sense of the number of M&M's in a bag of 65 (fractional parts of a set) and of the area of a square (fractional parts of a whole). As you can see, all four operations of addition, subtraction, multiplication, and division are used as the children think and reason mathematically, often by breaking the numbers into familiar components.

As we have surrounded ourselves with the concept of fractions, our homework has included the voices of many children in class as well. So far 19 of our 29 students have had their voices heard in our fraction homework.

Thanks for reading this lengthy epistle. I look forward to seeing you at conference time.

Sincerely,

Suzy Ronfeldt

Fraction Statements About 65 M&M's—Different Strategies

1. $\frac{1}{2}$ of 65 = 32$\frac{1}{2}$

   Martin: $\frac{1}{2}$ of 60 = 30 and $\frac{1}{2}$ of 5 = 2$\frac{1}{2}$ and 30 + 2$\frac{1}{2}$ = 32$\frac{1}{2}$.

2. $\frac{1}{4}$ of 65 = 16$\frac{1}{4}$

   Davida: 32$\frac{1}{2}$ is $\frac{1}{2}$ of 65 and 16$\frac{1}{4}$ + 16$\frac{1}{4}$ = 32$\frac{1}{2}$; therefore 16$\frac{1}{4}$ is $\frac{1}{4}$ of 65.

   Kevin: 32$\frac{1}{2}$ is $\frac{1}{2}$ of 65 and $\frac{1}{2}$ of 30 = 15; $\frac{1}{2}$ of 2$\frac{1}{2}$ = 1$\frac{1}{4}$ so 15 + 1$\frac{1}{4}$ = 16$\frac{1}{4}$.

   Anna: 16 + 16 + 16 + 16 = 64 and $\frac{1}{4}$ + $\frac{1}{4}$ + $\frac{1}{4}$ + $\frac{1}{4}$ = 1
   64 + 1 = 65.

   $$4 \times 16 = 64 \qquad 4 \times \tfrac{1}{4} = 1 \qquad 64 + 1 = 65$$

   Matt: 16$\frac{1}{4}$, 32$\frac{1}{2}$, 48$\frac{3}{4}$, 65.

3. $\frac{1}{8}$ of 65 = 8$\frac{1}{8}$

   Brooke: 16$\frac{1}{4}$ is $\frac{1}{4}$ of 65, so 16 ÷ 2 = 8 and $\frac{1}{4}$ ÷ 2 = $\frac{1}{8}$, so 8$\frac{1}{8}$.

   Annette: 65 ÷ 8 = 8 with 1 left over; 1 ÷ 8 = $\frac{1}{8}$; so 8 + $\frac{1}{8}$ = 8$\frac{1}{8}$.

   Penny: 8$\frac{1}{8}$ + 8$\frac{1}{8}$ = 16$\frac{1}{4}$ and 16$\frac{1}{4}$ is $\frac{1}{4}$ of 65; therefore 8$\frac{1}{8}$ is $\frac{1}{8}$ of 65.

4. $\frac{1}{16}$ of 65 = 4$\frac{1}{16}$

   Terry: I know 4 × 16 = 64 and $\frac{1}{16}$ × 16 = 1; therefore 64 + 1 = 65.

   Lisa: I know 8$\frac{1}{8}$ is $\frac{1}{8}$ of 65. Half of 8$\frac{1}{8}$ is 4$\frac{1}{16}$. I know 4 + 4 = 8 and $\frac{1}{16}$ + $\frac{1}{16}$ = $\frac{1}{8}$. Therefore 4 + $\frac{1}{16}$ = 4$\frac{1}{16}$.

   Alan: 8$\frac{1}{8}$ is $\frac{1}{8}$ of 65, 4 is $\frac{1}{2}$ of 8, and $\frac{1}{16}$ is $\frac{1}{2}$ of $\frac{1}{8}$; therefore 4$\frac{1}{16}$ is $\frac{1}{16}$ of 65.

5. $\frac{1}{5}$ of 65 = 13

   Mary: $\frac{1}{5}$ of 50 = 10 and $\frac{1}{5}$ of 15 = 3, so $\frac{1}{5}$ of 65 = 13.

   Ethan: 13 × 5 = 65 and 13, 26, 39, 52, 65, so 13 is $\frac{1}{5}$ of 65.

   Josh: 5 × 12 = 60 + 5 = 65; therefore 5 is $\frac{1}{13}$ of 65 because 5 × 13 = 65.

6. $\frac{1}{3}$ of 65 = 21$\frac{2}{3}$

   Matt: I skip counted 21$\frac{2}{3}$, 43$\frac{1}{3}$, 65.

   Penny: 60 ÷ 3 = 20, 5 ÷ 3 = 1$\frac{2}{3}$, and 20 + 1$\frac{2}{3}$ = 21$\frac{2}{3}$.

7. $\frac{3}{4}$ of 65 = 48$\frac{3}{4}$

   Annette: 32$\frac{1}{2}$ is $\frac{1}{2}$ of 65 and 16$\frac{1}{4}$ is $\frac{1}{4}$ of 65 so 32$\frac{1}{2}$ + 16$\frac{1}{4}$ = 48$\frac{3}{4}$.

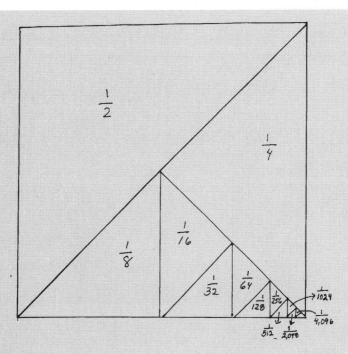

Josh's diagram.

Equations that you can prove by looking at the above design:

Hasan: $\frac{1}{8} + \frac{1}{16} + \frac{2}{32} = \frac{1}{4}$

Kevin: $\frac{1}{2} \div \frac{1}{16} = 8$

Lorrie: $\frac{1}{2} + \frac{1}{8} + \frac{1}{4} = \frac{7}{8}$

Martin: $\frac{1}{2} + \frac{2}{16} + \frac{1}{8} + \frac{1}{4} = 1$

Victor: $\frac{1}{4} + \frac{1}{2} + \frac{4}{8} = 1\frac{1}{4}$

Matt: $1 \div 4 = \frac{1}{4}$

Elena: $\frac{2}{4} + \frac{2}{8} + \frac{4}{16} = 1$

Mary: $\frac{1}{16} + \frac{2}{32} = \frac{1}{8}$

James: $\frac{3}{4} + \frac{4}{16} = 1$

Joni: $\frac{4}{32} + \frac{2}{16} + \frac{1}{8} = \frac{3}{8}$

Frankie: $\frac{1}{4} - \frac{1}{8} = \frac{1}{8}$

Annette: $\frac{4}{64} + \frac{1}{16} + \frac{1}{8} = \frac{1}{4}$

Kyle: $1 - \frac{3}{4} = \frac{1}{4}$

Davida: $\frac{2}{4} + \frac{4}{8} + \frac{8}{16} = 1\frac{1}{2}$

Moss: $\frac{1}{2} = \frac{2}{4} = \frac{8}{16}$

Brad: $\frac{1}{4} + \frac{2}{16} + \frac{1}{8} = \frac{1}{2}$

Ethan: $\frac{1}{8} + \frac{1}{8} + \frac{1}{4} = \frac{1}{2}$

Terry: $\frac{5}{512} = \frac{10}{1024} = \frac{20}{2048}$

Lisa: $\frac{1}{8} - \frac{2}{32} = \frac{1}{16}$

Chapter 2
Back-to-School Night

I've read that for most people the only thing more daunting than speaking in public is singing before an audience. It's little wonder that back-to-school night brings fear and trembling to almost every teacher I know. In addition to the butterflies inherent to speaking before a group, it's almost impossible to decide how to condense a year's worth of curriculum into a short presentation. It helps me to remember that on this night parents primarily want to know that I'm a reasonable person who cares about their children and is dedicated to teaching. When the night is over I let out a sigh of relief, knowing that the remainder of my interactions with parents are going to be in forums that feel much more comfortable to me.

Choosing Manipulatives

One of the first things that I do to get ready for back-to-school night is think about how I might help parents understand the role of manipulatives in the classroom. Adults who were taught mathematics primarily through the use of abstract symbols need the opportunity to make a connection between the mathematical ideas they encountered in school and the materials their children will be using. Seeing examples of manipulatives their children will use to represent mathematical ideas helps parents become more at ease with the new look of the mathematics program. Parents often become enthusiastic about manipulatives once they understand how the materials can help students develop concrete mental models of abstract concepts. They like the idea that their children will actually have some way to make mathematics meaningful and understandable.

Parents of first graders might benefit from seeing how cubes, tiles, and pattern blocks can be used to represent numbers. I might have on hand several Unifix cube trains, each eight cubes long and constructed of varying numbers of yellow and blue cubes. I might also set out children's designs made of eight toothpicks or eight pattern blocks. These constructions show how important it is for children to see the same number represented in many ways. Parents of third graders could be shown the ways that multiplication can be represented with concrete materials. The parents of older children need to see concrete representations of fractions. The important thing is to choose materials and concepts that match the curriculum the children will be experiencing during the year.

Choosing Student Work

At a back-to-school night a few years ago, almost as an afterthought, I showed some examples of work done by children who had been in my class the year before. Afterward, a parent remarked that this had been the most helpful part of my presentation. I've included examples of student work ever since.

When choosing student work, I try to find examples that best illustrate some of the major concepts we will be covering during the year. For instance, for first grade I show work that includes composing and decomposing numbers, because I want to illustrate the importance of that aspect of developing number sense. For second grade, I would choose work samples that involve solving story problems with two-digit numbers. For older grades, I would choose solutions for problems that require using multiplication, fractions, or percentages, depending on what I planned to work on that year. Sometimes I look for examples that illustrate increasingly efficient approaches to the same problem so that parents know that their children will be exposed to ideas that will encourage them to rethink their own less efficient solutions.

Whatever work I choose, my idea is to illustrate:

1. Some examples of the concepts covered at the particular grade level.

2. The ingenious and varied ways children go about making sense of mathematical ideas when they are given good problems to solve.

3. How important it is for the child to approach a problem in a way that makes sense to that child.

4. That we take time to share solutions in class so that the children can reexamine their own thinking in the light of how others solve problems.

Preparing the Environment

Before parents arrive I spend some time making sure that they'll be physically comfortable in the room. This includes making sure that there are enough seats for the number of people expected and that everyone will be able to see the materials I plan to present. I organize my materials by topic and make sure they're close at hand, usually on a table next to where I'll be speaking. If I'm going to use an overhead projector to show transparencies of children's work, I make sure it's focused on the screen. If possible I display student work on the walls, and I do a last-minute check to see that the room is tidy.

A few years ago my colleague Lianne Morrison told me that she asked each of her students to write a letter to his or her parents welcoming them to the classroom, then left these letters on the students' desks for the parents to read when they arrived at back-to-school night. I've started doing this too and find that it creates a positive feeling in the room that makes everyone, including me, feel more comfortable because it links all of us to the children. Even beginning-of-the-year first graders can be encouraged to write a few words to their parents. Asking students to tell something they like about school is a good way to help them focus their letters.

It's also great for the children to come in the next day to find brief letters from their parents, so I make sure there are paper and pencils available and give the parents time to write a brief note in return. (Children whose parents are unable to attend receive a note from me suggesting that we can mail their letters to their parents, along with any printed materials I handed out.)

Thinking Through What to Say

When I'm preparing what I'll say during the mathematics portion of my presentation, I zero in on a few major points I want to make. Most people can only take in a few big ideas at once, and I remind myself that I'm going to have many opportunities in the future, through newsletters, homework assignments, and conferences, to expand on the ideas I present at back-to-school night. Here's a list of the major ideas I try to get across:

1. *My goal is for your child to love and understand mathematics.* I want to present mathematics in a positive light. Some parents carry with them a backlog of negative feelings about math based on their own experiences in school. They've come to think of school math as a necessary evil—a subject that is inevitably painful. I find ways to talk about how in the past children often learned mathematics as a series of rules to be memorized, with little thought having been given to whether they understood the underlying mathematics. I emphasize that I'm committed to making sure that the children have experiences that reinforce the notion that mathematics makes sense and is intriguing. I explain briefly, "Your child is going to be playing games that are inherently interesting and solving problems that will encourage him or her to construct important understanding about mathematics."

2. *Appropriate materials will be available that will enable your child to explore the mathematical concepts studied at this grade level.* When I show examples of the manipulatives my students will use, I want the parents to understand that these materials are important learning tools. I don't necessarily downplay the notion that the materials are fun to work with, but I make sure parents see that the children will be using the materials to develop mathematical understanding. I emphasize the connection between the physical models the children construct with their hands and the mental models they construct in their heads. I make sure everyone can see the materials I've chosen, and I identify them loudly and clearly by name.

3. *Your child will be an active participant in the learning process.* The big idea here is that doing mathematics includes talking about it and writing about it. I want parents to know there will be many opportunities for their children to talk about mathematical ideas with me and with their classmates. I make sure I say that I've observed that putting their thinking in writing allows children to clarify that thinking. I strongly suggest that talking and writing about their mathematical thinking helps children become increasingly efficient problem solvers. Then, to support this point, I show a number of examples of work done by children, making sure their names have been deleted. I show a variety of solutions and emphasize the importance of the natural stages that children go through as they construct their understanding of complex mathematical ideas. (Appendix 2.1 includes four samples of student work I've used during back-to-school night, along with what I've said about them.) To conclude this portion of my introduction, I might say something like this: *The school's math program is designed to give children the experiences they will need in order to develop the kind of number sense this work exhibits. My goal is for the students to be able to handle all aspects of solving a problem—choosing the right numbers, choosing the right operations, performing the calculations, and evaluating the reasonableness of the answer. Real-life problems are nothing like the contrived, clearly delineated problems usually found in traditional workbooks.*

4. School mathematics may look different from the mathematics program you experienced as children because the world is changing. I like to touch briefly on the notion that students not only need to become proficient in arithmetic, they also need to be able to solve problems and to think flexibly. I mention that a good mathematics education must include experiences in geometry and data collection as well as in number sense. I emphasize that my goal is for my students to become people who think mathematically when approaching a variety of problems.

5. It's important to me and to your child that we form a partnership that supports your child's growth in mathematics. I explain that this is only a brief introduction to the math program and that there will be many opportunities for them to learn more about the math curriculum. I mention I'll be sending home newsletters that expand on the ideas that I'm introducing tonight. I tell them their children's homework assignments will give them additional insights into the mathematical ideas we're working on in class. Finally, I remind them that the parent-teacher conferences scheduled for later in the fall will give us an opportunity to talk about their child's individual progress. Because there generally isn't time to open the session up to questions and answers, I encourage parents to call me or write me a note if they have questions or concerns.

Responding to Difficult Questions

A back-to-school night is usually so tightly structured that I rarely have to face questions from highly critical parents. In any case, I much prefer to work with an unhappy parent one on one. So if a parent persists in asking questions that make me uncomfortable or that I am unable to answer, I suggest we discuss the issues at a separate meeting. So that the meeting will be as fruitful as possible, I ask the parent to jot down his or her most pressing concerns and send them to me, along with possible meeting dates and times. Knowing the specific concerns ahead of time enables me to prepare an honest and clear response.

Putting It All Together

If I've prepared thoroughly and well, the presentation itself usually goes smoothly. Right before I begin, I remind myself that this is my chance to share what I do well with a group of people who are eager to come away with a positive impression. When the moment of truth arrives and I'm faced with a roomful of eager parents, I try to speak with warmth and to convey my conviction that learning comes naturally to children. I want parents to think they might enjoy learning in this environment themselves. Sometimes a parent smiles and nods as I'm speaking, which gives me a wonderful boost. If no one is being visibly responsive, I imagine such a person in my mind's eye.

My first few sentences are occasionally a little shaky, but once I get going I can usually forget about myself. As I talk about the materials we'll be using and show examples of children's work, I recede into the background. The spotlight is on the children and the exciting time they are going to have learning during the coming year. More than once I've been disappointed to look up at the clock and realize I need to bring my talk to a close, which I do by saying something like this: *Your child came to school with a great deal of knowledge about mathematics, thanks to a natural curiosity about the world. And you have almost certainly played an integral part in helping your child develop mathematical concepts. Now I'm looking forward to joining you in the exciting job of nurturing and guiding your child as he or she continues the quest to make sense out of a very important part of our world—mathematics.* And then I happily let out that sigh of relief and head home for a bowl of ice cream!

APPENDIX 2.1
Examples of Student Work I've Shown to Parents on Back-to-School Night and What I've Said About It

I often ask my first graders to find multiple solutions to this problem: *If I want to put only red, yellow, and green crayons in a box, how many of each color do I need in order to have exactly 10 crayons in the box?* The children have red, yellow, and green cubes to use as they work. Here is Kris's solution.

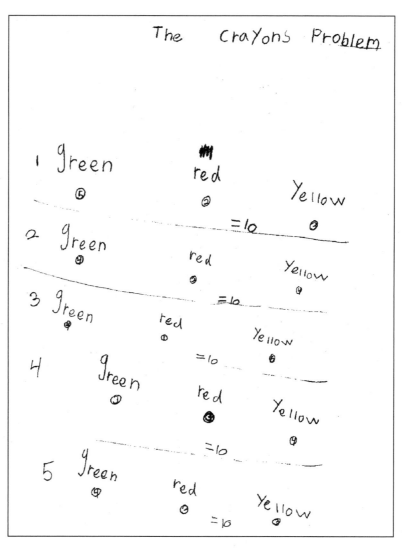

Kris used the cubes for her first few solutions and then put them aside as she added other possible solutions. Doing this kind of work helped Kris build important understanding about quantity. It also gave her experience with the notions that there can be many correct solutions to a problem and that perseverance is a part of mathematics. Her work is also an example of how the children are encouraged to record their answers in a format that is clear to others and makes sense to them.

The next two examples involve adding double-digit numbers. Before showing the student work, I'd probably try to engage the parents in some mathematical thinking: *Please double 29 in your head, paying attention not only to your answer but also to how you got your answer.* After a few moments I'd ask volunteers to describe their thinking. As they did, I'd record their ideas on the board. For example:

> 30 + 30 = 60 and then take away 2. That gives 58.
> 20 + 20 = 40 and 9 + 9 = 18. Then I added 40 + 18 to get 58.
> 9 + 9 = 18, put down the 8, carry the 1; 1 + 2 + 2 = 5 so my answer is 58.

After pointing out that there are a variety of reasonable ways to get the answer to this problem, I'd say that in the past students were often told that the only acceptable way to solve problems was the teacher's way. Then I would show the following pieces of work as evidence that students are also capable of coming up with reasonable strategies that made sense to them.

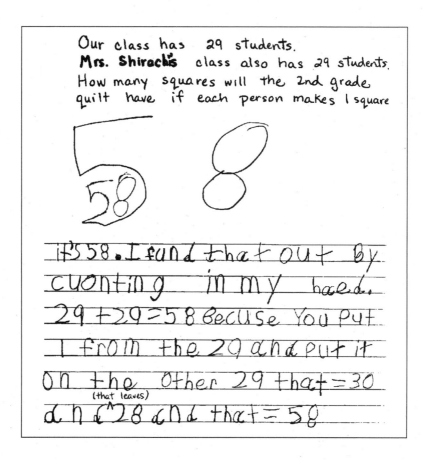

Our class has 29 students.
Mrs. Shirachis class also has 29 students.
How many squares will the 2nd grade
quilt have if each person makes 1 square

it's 58. I fund that out by
cuonting in my haed.
29 + 29 = 58 Becllse You Put
I from the 29 and Put it
on the Other 29 that = 30
(that leaves)
and 28 and that = 58

This child was able to use the notion of friendly numbers to solve
the problem 29 + 29. He quickly changed the problem to 30 + 28
so that he could figure out the answer in his head.

This boy took another approach:

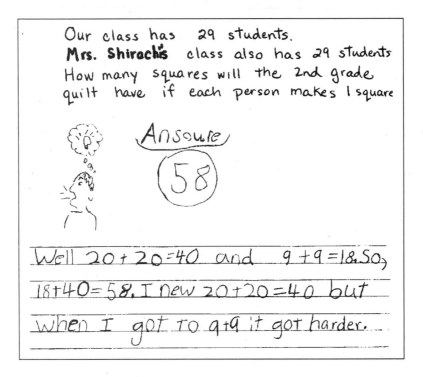

Our class has 29 students.
Mrs. Shirachi's class also has 29 students
How many squares will the 2nd grade
quilt have if each person makes I square

Ansoure
(58)

Well 20 + 20 = 40 and 9 + 9 = 18. So,
18 + 40 = 58. I new 20 + 20 = 40 but
when I got to 9 + 9 it got harder.

He decomposed each of the 29s into a 20 and a 9. He then added the two 20s to get 40, added the two 9s to get 18, and combined the 40 and the 18 to get 58.

Early in the year, most second graders solve these kinds of problems by counting. These examples are from later in the year when the children have moved on to being able to chunk numbers together to solve problems more efficiently. The important thing to note is that children, too, are very capable of coming up with solutions that make sense *if* they're given opportunities to develop understanding about our number system. We build number sense in class by playing number games, building mathematical models with manipulatives, solving problems, and talking about those solutions.

Ms. Mcrady earns $16.50 an hour as a welder. How much does she earn in an 8 hour day?

She earns $132

The way that I got this was by adding 16+16=32 then 32x2=64 then 64x2=128. Then I did half of 8 because 50¢ and got 4 dollars And, I added that to $128 and got $132.

This example is taken from a multiplication unit for upper-grade students. This child was able to decompose the $16.50 hourly wage into units that were easy to work with—$16 and 50 cents. She then used the notion that multiplication is repeated addition to account for the eight units of $16. She was very comfortable doubling numbers and knew when to stop. Notice also the mental manipulation she used to find out how to include the eight units of 50 cents. She used her knowledge that 50 cents is half of a dollar to come up with the $4.00 she needed to add to her solution. It took her a while to write down her thinking, but my guess is that she actually got the answer very quickly using her method. This solution is an accurate and efficient way to solve this problem.

▼ ▼ ▼

Chapter 3
Parent Conferences

Holding conferences with parents has a deserved reputation for being time-consuming and emotionally demanding. The high-stakes quality of conferences is inherent to the situation: both teacher and parents care deeply about the child they are discussing and feel a high degree of responsibility for that child's success as a student and as a person. Finding a way to tap into this high degree of caring in a relaxed and positive way is important, because conferences are a rare commodity—a time and place to focus on the needs and abilities of each child as an individual. I try to use a conference to get to know my students better: I carefully review their work beforehand and ask the parents to be active participants. Ideally, teacher and parents pour equal effort into the conference, firming up the notion of a parent-teacher partnership. A conference gives me a chance to show parents that I'm knowledgeable about their children and that I'm open to any ideas and information the parents have. Most of all, I see a conference as an opportunity to celebrate the many strengths and abilities of each of my students.

Encouraging Parents to Be Active Participants

Parents have a wealth of information about their child, based on years of knowing and caring deeply for her or him. Whatever the ultimate thrust of the conference may be, they will be better focused and have more to contribute if they have had some time to think about their role beforehand.

Therefore, a few weeks before the conference is to take place, I send a note to parents explaining that I see them as their child's first and most important teacher. I ask them to be prepared to tell me about their child's interests and strengths. I suggest that they consider whether there are any problems related to their child's development they feel I should know about and what their goals for their child are for the current school year. The letter I send home is short and goes something like this:

Dear Room 5 Families,

I look upon the upcoming parent-teacher conferences as a great opportunity for us to learn from one another.

As part of the conference I'll be sharing some of the work that your child has done during the previous report period. I'll also talk about my observations of your child's growth as a student. I hope my comments will help you expand your understanding of your child.

This conference is also an opportunity for me to learn from you. You've known, loved, and observed your child for a number of years now. You are and will continue to be your child's first and most important teacher. You have a wealth of information about him or her as a person and as a learner. I'm especially interested in hearing from you about your child's strengths and interests. This will also be a good time to let me know about any problems or goals you feel I should know about.

I look forward to meeting with you.

Sincerely,

Nancy

Taking this idea a step further, my colleague Suzanne Latham, at the very beginning of the school year, tells her students' parents that they're welcome to send her a letter describing their child. The parents who take her up on this offer have a wonderful chance to reflect on who their child is. They love being able to describe the great things about their child. Suzanne says that parents who are anxious about some aspect of their child's development or previous school experience find this opportunity especially useful. When I've suggested this to the parents of my students, the letters I've received have been treasures. Suzanne suggests returning the letters to the parents at the end of the year so that they can go into the family archives.

Scheduling Conferences

As part of my note announcing the conference, I also ask parents to let me know the times that are most convenient for them. I generally send home a list of all the available times and ask them to cross out those that are not possible. (See the sample form in Figure 3.1.) I make sure to specify a date by when I need to receive this scheduling information, generally about a week from when I make the request.

When I have everyone's responses, I sit down and make a master calendar, scheduling each family into a slot that works for them. (This sometimes involves making special arrangements with parents who, because of work or family circumstances, cannot meet at any of the scheduled times, which are determined by my district.) When I know a particular conference is likely to need a little extra time, I try to schedule it at the end of a day so we can run over the usual half hour. Or I might schedule a particularly demanding conference early in the day so I'll be fresh. Once the master calendar is set up I fill out a form for each family letting them know the exact time they are scheduled to come.

Other teachers find that it works to put out a sign-up sheet at back-to-school night. However, I like having some control over when particular conferences are scheduled, so I prefer my method. The important thing to remember is that parents need to have a voice in when they are scheduled to appear.

One of my most embarrassing moments occurred one day when I had far too many conferences, scheduled one right after

Dear Room 5 Families,

Indicated below are the times when I am scheduling parent conferences. CROSS OUT ALL
THE TIMES YOU ARE UNABLE TO COME. Please return this note by Monday, March 16.

I'll let you know the exact time of your conference as soon as possible.

Nancy

CROSS OUT THE TIMES WHEN YOU CANNOT COME.

Tuesday, March 31		Thursday, April 12		Friday, April 13		
8:00	1:00	8:00	1:00	7:30	10:00	1:00
	1:30		1:30	8:00	10:30	1:30
	2:00		2:00	8:30	11:00	2:00
	2:30		2:30	9:00	11:30	2:30

YOUR NAME: _____   YOUR CHILD: _____

FIGURE 3.1. ▲ Conference scheduling form.

the other. I was talking about a child with his parents and called him by the wrong name. For years I had feared making just such a mistake, so it was almost a relief to do it and discover that I could survive the embarrassment. Nevertheless, I would just as soon not have it happen again. So I now make sure to build some break time into every conference day. I can personally handle four conferences in a row with just a brief time between each one in which to flip through the next child's stack of work, but I schedule at least a twenty-minute break before I start on conference number five.

Before the Conference Begins

Before the first set of parents arrive, I make sure I've arranged a comfortable corner of the classroom with adult-sized chairs to accommodate the number of people who are likely to show up. I like to be able to see a clock easily, so I can keep track of time without being too obvious.

I gather together all the materials I plan to share during that day's conferences and put each child's stack in order according to what should be presented first, second, and so on. I spread these stacks across a table or counter so that each child's work is at my fingertips when I need it.

I make sure I have on hand a glass of water for myself and a box of tissues. Conferences are demanding for me and may also be stressful for some parents. Just being in a classroom can bring back old memories, some of them negative. Divorced parents may have the added burden of interacting with a former partner with whom they are not comfortable. One of my most uncomfortable moments during a conference occurred when a child's mother suddenly jumped up and ran out of the room in tears. Her husband then explained that they had just separated. I was relieved to know the hasty departure had nothing to do with me, but carrying on wasn't easy. I would have liked a swallow of something a little stronger than water!

Finally, I remind myself that parents who are particularly anxious about their child may sometimes let their emotions take over and resort to unproductive attacks on some aspect of their child's schooling. I'm mentally prepared to end the conference should this happen. I would tell the parents that the discussion was not serving the best interest of their child and that a meeting including the school principal (or other supportive school personnel) could be arranged at a later date. I've never had to resort to this position, but I rest easier knowing that I have a plan in reserve that will preserve everyone's dignity.

The Conference

My cardinal rule is to begin every conference on a positive note. I generally mention some recent triumph the child has experienced at school or some especially endearing quality she or he has exhibited. This friendly beginning conveys to parents that I like and appreciate their child. It makes parents feel at ease and gives them confidence that I have their child's best interest at heart. They are also more likely to be receptive to any problems I may need to discuss later in the conference.

After I've set this positive tone, I ask the parents to tell me about their child. I help them focus by reminding them that I'm interested in hearing about their child's strengths and interests. As I listen to their description, I pay attention not only to the information they provide but also to what they leave out. I get them to round out their story by asking a question or two. I learn a lot about what parents value and how they relate to their children from what they say. Sometimes parents want to get right to the things they see as problems. I listen to these concerns, but I also make sure that the conference includes plenty of time to share positive thoughts about the child. I want to help parents appreciate their child's good qualities.

Listening attentively as parents talk sends the message that I appreciate their all-important role in the education of their child. It also tells them that I am deeply interested in their child's growth. Parents probably aren't often asked to blow their horns about their child's unique qualities, and most parents relish the chance to do so.

If parents mention a particular educational goal, I take specific notes so that I can follow up on it throughout the year. If the goal is unrealistic—having a first grader memorize the multiplication table by the end of the year, for example—I try to respond to the underlying concern, which is that their child encounter a rigorous math curriculum. I let them know that I recognize and share their interest in skill development. I might even describe how I'll be helping my students become more proficient with numbers, at the same time emphasizing how important it is for children to understand what they're doing in mathematics. (I'll also make a note to myself that I need to send out a newsletter that describes how number sense is developed.) In any case, discussions like this remind me that I need to let parents know what I consider to be developmentally appropriate for their children.

After thanking the parents for their perspective, I offer some thoughts about how my perception of their child matches or contrasts with theirs. Then I begin showing the samples of student work I've collected, explaining what the work tells about the child's growth. (A little later I discuss some ideas about how to choose student work to share during a conference.) For example, look at first grader Lana's solution to the Rooster problem, shown in Figure 3.2. Here's what I told Lana's parents:

Sometimes a piece of literature can be an interesting context for problem solving. I had read aloud *Rooster's Off to See the World* [Eric Carle, Scholastic, 1972], a one-to-five counting book that involves one rooster, two cats, and so on up to five fish who go on a journey. The problem I posed for the children to solve was, *How many animals went off to see the world?* You can see that Lana got the correct answer and that she's been very clear about how she solved the problem through counting. Her work shows that she has a good conceptual understanding of what the problem entails. She made a point of using pictures, tally marks, and numbers to solve the problem. She counted accurately, an important skill for a first grader when working in the mathematical strand of number. When she brought her paper up to me, it was very important to her that I notice how complete she had been. This is just one example of what a conscientious student Lana is. When I asked Lana to share

FIGURE 3.2.▲ Lana's work.

her paper with the class, I noticed that the other children also took note of how complete she had been. On subsequent problems that the children have been asked to solve, I've noticed that her work has served as a good example for some of her classmates.

If I had omitted showing the student work and just described Lana as "well organized and always eager to do her best work," her parents would have been reassured, but they wouldn't have seen how these characteristics play out for Lana when she's doing mathematics. Being able to back my statements up with a look at how Lana actually organized her thoughts on paper in solving a real problem gives a much fuller picture, both of Lana's way of working and what we are doing in the math program.

For any work I share, I take pains to describe the context of the problem and to mention the strand of mathematics it falls under. Then, when I go on to describe how their child approached the problem, parents can better understand why the work is significant. In addition to describing the actual mathematical thinking that went into the work, I make sure to include my observations about the child's attitude toward doing mathematics, ability to organize thinking, and willingness to persevere in the face of difficulty. I explain that children who are committed to working hard on problems, even those that are difficult, are learning the tools that will help them throughout their mathematics career.

If I've had a chance to do an individual assessment (this is also discussed in more detail later), I discuss the observations I made during the assessment interview and explain what they tell me about the child's growth. My comments on an assessment interview with a second grader about her understanding of place value might go something like this:

I asked Tilly to organize 24 cubes into groups of 10s and extras and to use the groups to figure out how many cubes there were altogether. After creating two groups of 10 and a group of 4 extras, she explained that 10 plus 10 makes 20 and went on to count the 4 extras by 1s to come up with an accurate total of 24. Most second graders feel comfortable and are accurate doing this task. I then told Tilly that I wanted only 16 cubes. "What do you need to do so that there are exactly 16 cubes on the table?" It's not at all unusual for a second grader to start from scratch, counting out 16 cubes, one at a time. Tilly, however, pulled one group of 10 closer to her, commenting that this gave her 10 so far, then she added the group of 4 extras, saying, "Now I've got 14." She then added 2 additional cubes to bring the total quantity up to 16. She pushed aside the remaining 8 cubes. I inferred from observing Tilly that she is comfortable working with chunks of numbers and is able to conserve numbers of this size. This ability to conserve number—to know that she had a group of 10 without recounting it cube by cube—is crucial to being able to add and subtract numbers. I then went on to ask Tilly to write the number 16, which she also did handily. I next asked her some questions to see whether she was able to relate the quantity of cubes on the table to the symbols we use to represent that quantity. . . .

I would continue in this fashion, describing both the mathematical information that I've gathered and what my observations have suggested to me about the child's organizational skills and confidence level, always trying to help parents understand the complexity of the mathematics involved from the child's point of view.

I conclude the conference by relaying any concerns I have, and if I can I suggest games or activities parents can do at home to help a child who needs more experiences with a particular concept. Once again, I end on a positive note, letting the parents know that I appreciate what they have to say and that I enjoy working with their child.

Most parents appreciate the time and effort that goes into a conference, but I try to maintain the attitude that even parents who are negative do care about their child's learning. That way I'm less annoyed by questions that seem to come out of left field. When parents express dissatisfaction about some aspect of their child's schooling, sometimes quiet, nonjudgmental listening is the best course of action. When parents bring up a sore point, gently asking, *Why is that important?* in an even tone can help them clarify their own thinking and can sometimes lead to common ground. The important thing is not to get defensive and to maintain a professional distance that allows everyone to maintain his or her dignity.

Happily, most conferences are not adversarial. Parents are likely to leave the conference feeling positive about their child's school experience and grateful to have received so much specific information about their child. I leave the conference having learned a great deal about the child and therefore being better prepared for my teaching role. I'm enormously relieved when that final conference is over but also invigorated by my contact with parents and by the knowledge I have gained.

Choosing Student Work to Share at Conferences

I know that having samples of the child's efforts will give the parents and me something concrete on which to focus our attention. While describing the way their child has gone about solving a specific problem, I'll be able to comment on his or her mathematical thinking in a lively way that includes the child's attitude toward doing mathematics. Having a little piece of the child there in the room can even dissipate some of the natural uneasiness we may all be feeling. And the student work allows me to give a fuller picture of what math looks like in my classroom.

I begin preparing a few months ahead by setting aside class sets of children's work. For example, I might ask my second graders to use words, pictures, and/or symbols to show how they would solve a word problem that involves addition. I then collect each child's paper to make up the class set, making sure that the children have dated their papers. On another day I might ask each child to solve a problem connected to a story we've read. These papers make up a second class set of children's work.

When I'm ready to make choices, I take out the class sets of problems I've put aside. If I haven't already reviewed the work carefully, I divide *each class set* into three piles: work that shows evidence of strong understanding, work that can be characterized as being on grade level, and work that indicates the child is confused or has little access to the problem. As I divide each set of papers into these three piles, I look for patterns, noting who consistently turns up in the first or third category. In this way, I begin to get a clearer picture in my own mind of how my students are growing mathematically over time (here's where having dates on the papers helps tremendously). This process also generally helps me clarify which problems will offer the most information to parents.

After I've chosen the problem(s) I want to share during the conferences, I jot down some notes characterizing each child's work and accurately describing her or his mathematical development. I want to be able to recall as many details as I can about what happened for that particular child solving that particular problem. I also think about what I might say to parents about why this work is significant mathematically.

Figure 3.3 is an example of how a second grader solved the problem 35 + 27. In this instance I did not have a context for the numbers. Instead, I asked the children to solve the equation and then write a story that matched the equation.

Here are my notes about Natasha's solution: *She is much more sure of herself when presenting this solution than she has been in the past—how exciting to see her confidence growing. She's still at the stage where she needs to use tallies, and counting is her main strategy, but she's starting to use groups of ten—another first. She does what kids typically do—adds the tens first and then the ones— but this is a natural and efficient way to solve this problem. She didn't have time to do the second part of the assignment, which was to write a story to go with the equation. But she does use words to clearly de- scribe how she solved the problem.* Since time is of the essence in teaching, sometimes, of course, these notes are mental rather than written—the important thing is that I've thought about the child and his or her work and these thoughts will be triggered when I see the work again.

Choosing work for conferences enables me to reinforce my deep-seated convictions about the way I am teaching mathemat- ics. It also helps me become clearer about the choices I'm making in general for my students. For example, when I look at George's solution to the 35 + 27 problem (see Figure 3.4), I'm reminded of how important it is to present open-ended problems to my stu-

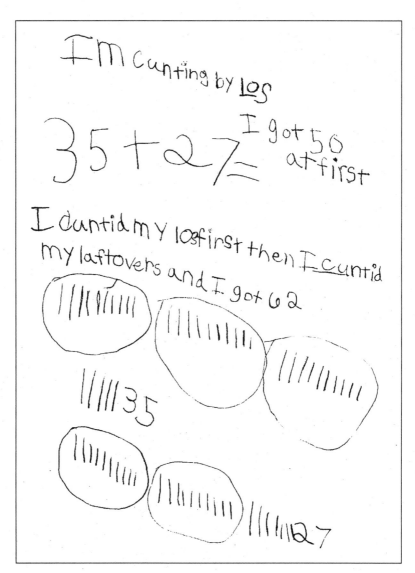

FIGURE 3.3.▲ Natasha's solution to 35 + 27.

dents. I would never have known that George was so gifted mathematically if he spent his time doing pages of double-digit addition. George was able to solve the addition problem *and* explain
the steps that he used for his mathematical solution *and* create a
story context that matched the original problem. He then went on

thirty five plus twenty seven = sixty two
once apon a time. There were thirty five orange peels.
on the ground. And twenty seven orange peels
on the table. then six spiders came. and one of the
spider said. "There are thirty five orange peels on the ground
and twenty seven on the table. How
many orande pleals do we get?" one of the spider
said. Thirty five plus twenty seven = sixty two. Because
thirty plus twenty = fifty. and five plus seven = twelve.
and fifty plus twelve = sixty two.
so there are sixty two orange peals.
and there are five plus me = six. so we
each get ten . And plus me = six. so we
we cut one of they two the two left over
peals. And we do this into three orange
peal. The end. so my idea was that. other orange
peal.

FIGURE 3.4. ▲ George's solution to 35 + 27.

to create a new problem (how to share the orange peels equally among the six spiders) and solve it accurately as well. When I talked with George's parents about his work, it was clear to all of us that George was being challenged by our math program in the best way possible: he was challenging himself, taking every opportunity to extend and articulate his thinking.

Actually, I try to evaluate student work periodically even when I'm not preparing for conferences. My hectic teaching schedule gives me very little time for reflection about my students or the curriculum choices I'm making. The daily math lesson is followed by the daily writing lesson and then it's on to another subject. I need to force myself to slow down and regularly review the work children are doing so that I can make good curriculum choices and choose good organizational strategies. It's a good thing that preparing for conferences forces me to undertake this process, but I try to repeat it at several other times during the year.

After I've reviewed the children's work (Appendix 3.1 contains some additional examples), I'm better prepared to think about both the general direction my math program should be taking and what I might try in order to provide for the individual needs of particular students. I might decide, for example, that it's time to move on to a new unit of study because most of the kids have demonstrated that they understand the concepts we've covered. Or it might be clear that I need to give the children more problems like the ones we've been working on because so many of them appear to be on the verge of new understanding. In this case, my review will also tell me to whom I need to pay special attention. I can think through the kinds of questions that might help a particular student develop new understanding. Or I may decide to bring together a small group of children who seem to be having problems, working with them as the other children work independently.

Individual Assessments

In addition to sharing student work with parents, I also like to be prepared to discuss my observations from an individual assessment interview I've conducted with each child. For example, in first grade, I might take a close look at individual counting strategies by setting up tasks for each child to perform. I might use one task to see if a child uses the strategy of counting on. A different task would give evidence of how many objects a child can count accurately using one-to-one correspondence. I've found Kathy Richardson's videotape series *A Look at Children's Thinking* (see resources) particularly helpful when I'm devising individual interviews for assessing counting abilities in kindergarten through second grade.

In second grade, place value might be the focus of an interview. Math By All Means, *Place Value, Grades 1–2*, by Marilyn Burns

(Math Solutions Publications, 1994), includes a section on individual interviews to assess beginning place value understanding.

Individual interviews help me feel connected to and knowledgeable about each child. Often, parents are reassured to know I've looked so carefully at their child's thinking and reasoning. And hearing about the tasks on which the assessment interview is based helps parents appreciate the intricacy of the mathematical ideas their child is studying, helps them realize that mathematical understanding is complex and highly individual. Discussing these interviews often serves as a starting point for getting parents to realize what they can do at home to support mathematical growth.

It can be difficult to find the time to sit down for an interview with each child. I'm able to work with individual students fairly regularly by establishing a routine period of the day, which I call Project Time, generally lasting thirty or forty minutes. During this time, which I schedule at least three days a week, the children, individually or in self-chosen small groups, are free to work with any of the materials in the classroom: exploring a variety of manipulatives; drawing; reading; writing; or playing games. (Project Time also gives the children a chance to practice independent decision making. I sometimes tell parents it's preparation for graduate school!) The rules governing the period are a reiteration of our basic class rules: be friendly with one another, take care of materials both during the work period and at clean-up time, use time wisely. I am then free to call a child aside for a one-on-one interview.

Student-Parent Conferences

Teachers aren't the only ones who can confer effectively with parents. Sometimes, students can do the best job of letting parents know what's happening in math class. Sessions at which children share their own work can take place at home or at school.

Maryann Wickett regularly enlists her students' help in reviewing work and reporting progress. Here's how she goes about it. After her class has completed a unit of study, each of Maryann's students reviews the work he or she has completed. As part of this review, each child chooses three pieces of work to include in a math portfolio. Each of the three pieces must represent at least one of five categories:

1. The child's best work.

2. A favorite paper.

3. A paper that describes a mathematical discovery or theory.

4. A paper that clearly explains mathematical thinking.

5. A paper dealing with an idea about which the student is still wondering or unsure.

The children then write about why they've chosen the three pieces. They also reflect on their work in a more general way. (Maryann has created forms the children can use to organize this reflective writing; see the examples in Appendix 3.2.) The completed portfolio consists of:

1. A cover letter to parents from Maryann.

2. The three pieces of math work.

3. The child's two reflective pieces of writing.

The children then take their portfolio home and share it with their parents. The parents are encouraged to comment about what they learned from this process and to write to Maryann about any questions they have. Appendix 3.2 is the portfolio Helen took home after she had completed a unit on division.

I use a similar process with my first and second graders in the spring of the year, but instead of taking their work home, my students conduct a conference at school, one that touches on all subjects. During the math portion, the children teach their parents a new math game and together they solve some problems. For example, if the class is in the middle of a probability unit, the child and her or his parents sample cubes from a sock and figure out what colors of cubes are in the sock. Or if we're in the middle of a geometry unit, parents and child work at adding another shape or color arrangement to our four-triangle chart. The idea is to let the parents experience firsthand what their children are studying in class. (For more information about making student-led conferences successful, see Austin 1994 in the resources bibliography.)

Students, parents, and teachers all benefit when student voices are included in the reporting process. My young students are thrilled to be in charge and to have their parents' undivided attention, something that happens rarely in these fast-paced times. Most parents love seeing their children in this leadership role. They like having a format for positive and open interaction with their children around school learning. Teachers are well aware of the value of having their students review and reflect on their own learning, and they enjoy knowing that attention is being directed where it should be—on student growth.

APPENDIX 3.1
Examples of Children's Work[1] to Share and the Type of Comments That Might Be Useful

[1]Work identified with an asterisk was provided by Maryann Wickett.

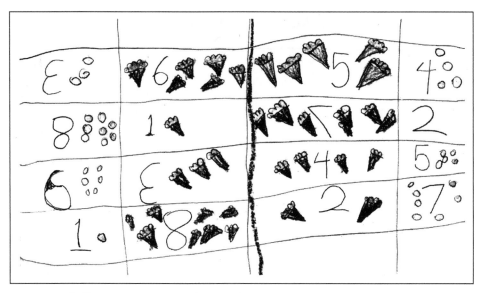

Megan's work (first grade, beginning of the year).

This is Megan's solution to the problem, *If you had 9 in all, and some are peas and some are carrots, how many of each kind of vegetable could you have?* Her work is well organized and accurate. She was persistent and actually found all the possible solutions. She used pictures to help her keep track of the numbers and identified the groups with numbers. This problem gave Megan experience with the number combinations that make up 9, but even more important, it was an opportunity to explore the concept that a number can be decomposed into smaller numbers. This is one of the big ideas in understanding how our number system works. Megan will be encountering and using this idea as she solves many problems in the future.

Megan's work (first grade, a few days later).

A few days after Megan did the peas and carrots problem, she was asked to think of her own category (she chose slices of cheese pizza and slices of pepperoni pizza) for the 11-in-all problem. In this work, Megan no longer needed to make pictures of each slice of pizza. She used the numbers to represent the quantities and did the thinking in her head. She didn't find all the possible solutions, but her work is impressive for a beginning first grader working with a relatively large number.

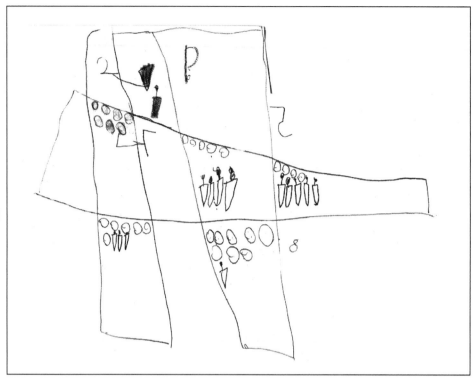

Andrea's work (first grade, beginning of the year).

When Andrea worked on the peas and carrots problem for 9, she needed my support. After she had come up with one or two solutions, she was stuck. I asked her to tell me about her first solution and then prompted, "How many peas could you have next time?" She decided on 5 peas and then was able to use drawings to keep track of how many carrots she would need to add. Sometimes a simple question that encourages a student to reflect on her work is all that's needed to help her move on. Andrea will have lots of opportunities this year to solve problems that will encourage her to be an independent thinker. I also notice that Andrea has put effort into organizing her work by creating a system of boxes for each solution. Organization isn't easy for Andrea, but she's beginning to expand on her work by labeling some of the groups of peas and carrots with numbers. This problem gave Andrea the opportunity to see that a number can be decomposed into smaller numbers, an idea that she'll encounter and use in many problem situations.

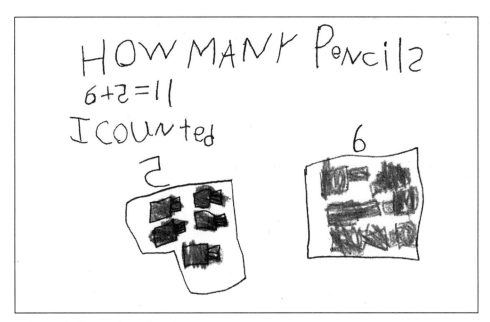

Kyle's work (first grade, midyear).

This is Kyle's solution to a story problem about finding 6 pencils at the back of the room and 5 more in another spot. I told the students they could choose materials in the room to help them solve the problem and that they should show their thinking on paper using words, pictures, and/or numbers. Kyle used cubes to represent the pencils, and as he has indicted, he then counted the cubes. Counting is an important activity for first graders; it helps them develop a sense of quantity. Kyle has clearly understood the problem, knows he has to combine the two quantities, and has made a record of his thinking. He even added an equation that represents the story problem. When he brought his paper to me initially, he hadn't included the pictures of the cubes. I asked him how he had figured out the answer, and he explained about organizing the cubes and then counting them. I asked him to complete his paper by drawing the cubes, and this work is the result: a paper that does a great job of fulfilling the requirements of the assignment. When the class met to discuss the various ways class members went about solving this problem, Kyle was eager to share his method.

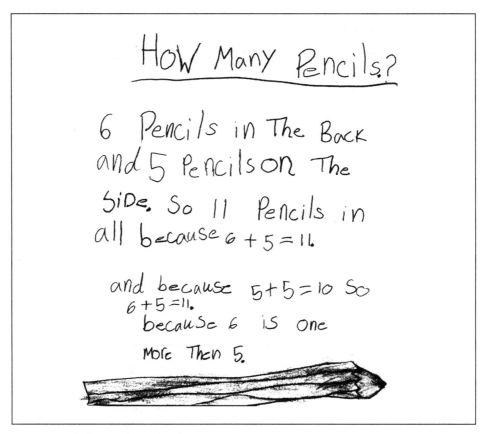

How Many Pencils?

6 Pencils in The Back and 5 Pencils on The Side. So 11 Pencils in all because 6 + 5 = 11.

and because 5+5=10 So 6+5=11. because 6 is one more Then 5.

Megan's work (first grade, midyear).

This is Megan's way of solving the same problem. Her work reveals how she goes about solving a combining problem by using her knowledge of number relationships. When she first brought her paper to me, it stopped midway down the page ("So 11 pencils in all because 6 + 5 = 11"). I reminded her that I wanted to know what she did to get her solution, that I was interested in her thinking. To give her a little nudge, I asked, "How could you prove that 6 + 5 = 11?" She explained how she had used her knowledge that 5 plus 5 equals 10 to figure out the answer. She went on to write out her thinking, and we later talked about how her work was now clear and complete. Being able to communicate about mathematical ideas is an important goal of our math program; Megan is off to a great start. She was very eager to share her thinking with others when the class met to discuss different strategies for solving this problem.

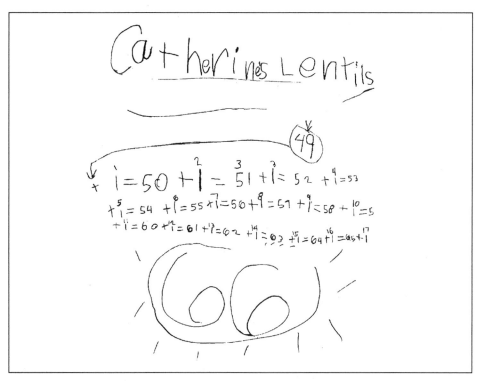

Boris's work (second grade).

This is Boris's solution to a problem in which I explained to the children that a girl named Catherine, in another class, had been asked to estimate how many lentils it would take to fill a cube. Catherine estimated 49, but when she counted the lentils in her cube, she discovered that she had a group of 49 and a group of 17. The problem was to figure out how many lentils she had used altogether to fill the cube. Boris understood the situation and approached the problem by counting on. He was meticulous about keeping track of the 17 ones that he needed to add to 49. His work is complete. Over the course of our unit working with large numbers, Boris will have many opportunities to solve problems involving large numbers. He'll be counting and playing games that give him experience with quantities this size. He'll have a chance to listen to other students describe their strategies for solving problems. He'll become increasingly efficient at combining larger quantities. For now, it's great that he's able to come up with a workable plan to solve this problem. His approach is grade appropriate, and he described what he did clearly.

Catherine's   lentils

I think there 66 lentils
becus she counted

49 + 10 = 59   59 + 7 = 66

there are 66 lentils.
you now there are
59. if it was 60 then
it wuld be 67. but
59 + 7 = 66 so it is 66.

Ted's work (second grade).

In this solution to the lentils problem, we see how Ted's understanding of de-composing numbers really pays off. By decomposing 17 into 10 and 7, he hand-ily moves from 49 to 59 to 66. I love the way he does the second calculation, explaining how he knew that $59 + 7 = 66$. He first thinks about a friendly num-ber (by changing 59 to 60), which makes it easy to add the 7 (67). He then drops back one to 66, to account for the difference between 59 and 60. These mental calculations show a depth of understanding about our number system that will serve Ted well throughout his life. It takes time to write out the think-ing involved, but the actual calculation happened quickly and was an efficient way to solve this problem. Ted never lost track of the quantities involved and was very clear in his written explanation. In class, we make sure that the chil-dren have a chance to share their solutions. Ted's solution may spark others to reexamine their own thinking, and Ted will also have a chance to see how others come up with equally efficient, but different, solutions to problems.

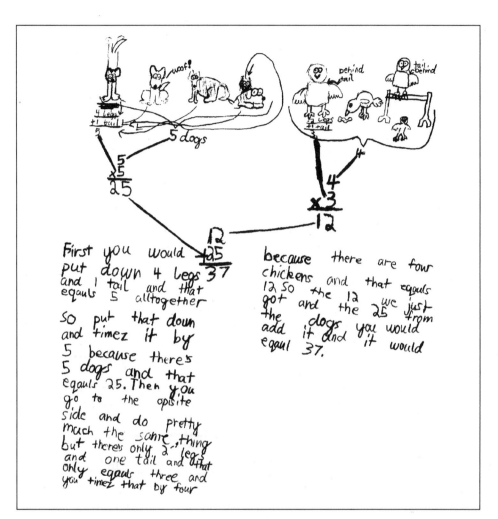

Sean's work* (fourth grade).

How many legs and tails would there be if you had 5 dogs and 4 chickens? Sean's
solution shows how well organized he is in his presentation of the problem,
how well he understands the situation, and how he is able to use his computational skills for both multiplication and addition to get an accurate solution.
He sets up the problem clearly with his drawings, uses equations to work out
the numbers, and writes out a narrative that makes his thinking crystal clear.
He's shown both mathematical ability and communications skills in this piece
of work. He's meeting many important standards of the mathematical program.

```
 3
 8
13
18
23
28
33
38
43
48
53
58
63
68
73
78
83
88
93
103
108
193
118
123
128
133
```

1. In the ones colamn the pattern is 3, 8, 3, 8, 3, 8, 3, 8, ect.

2. In the tens colamn the pattern is, 0, 0, 1, 1, 2, 2, 3, 3, 4, 4, 5, 5, 6, 6, 7, 7, ect.

3. , If you take out all the ones with 8 you are skiping ten.

4. The numbers go odd, even, odd, even, odd, ect.

Reflection: I wonder if I did this up t 1003 how many numbers would I have. I think it would be 210 becouse it tskes 21 to get to 103 then you would multiplie by ten becouse there is ten hundretts in 1000.

Allison's work* (fourth grade).

This work grew out of a unit on patterning. Looking for patterns helps children make sense out of mathematics and is an underlying principle of mathematics. Allison used a calculator and recorded what happened when she added 5 to 3. She then used the plus key to continue adding 5 to each previous sum. She's come up with several observations about the ensuing numeric pattern. Her reflection shows that she is able to apply the important mathematical concept that patterns allow one to predict beyond the particular. Planners in many different fields use this idea when analyzing data. It's significant also to note that she comes up with her own next problem. When she wonders about how many numbers she would have if she continued the pattern to 1003, she's showing that she's involved in her work. She also shows a good understanding of our number system when she works out the answer to her question. She knows that she needs to multiply 21 by 10 because she understands the relationship of 100 to 1000.

Amber's work* (fourth grade).

Amber did this problem as part of a unit on division. She was asked to explain her thinking about sharing $5.00 equally among four friends. Amber is efficient in her solution and also communicates her thinking clearly through words, pictures, and numbers. This problem gives her an opportunity to see how division relates to the real world. There are many different ways to arrive at a correct solution to this problem; her very efficient method enabled her to make a significant contribution to the class discussion about ways to solve this problem. Amber's solution shows how multiplication and repeated addition relate to division.

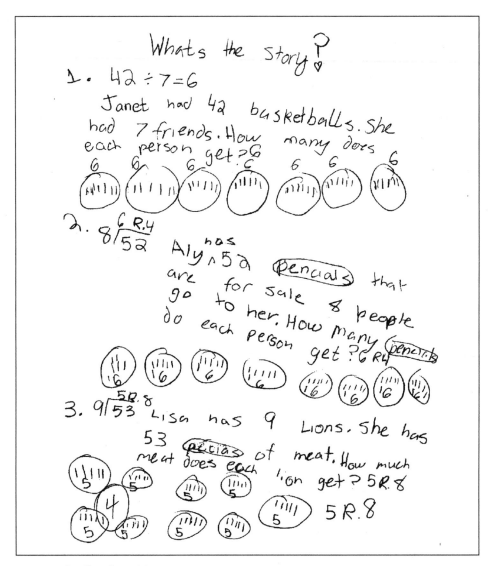

What's the story?

1. 42 ÷ 7 = 6

Janet had 42 basketballs. She had 7 friends. How many does each person get? 6

6   6   6   6   6   6   6

2. 8)52 6 R.4

Aly has 52 pencials that are for sale 8 people go to her. How many pencils do each person get? 6 R4

6   6   6   6   6   6   6   6

3. 9)53 5R.8

Lisa has 9 Lions. She has 53 pecias of meat. How much meat does each lion get? 5R.8

5   5   5   5   5   4   5   5   5   5   5R.8

Amy's work* (fourth grade).

This work was part of a unit on division. It's important that students understand that numeric problems relate to the real world. Requiring children to solve story problems gives them a chance to think through the situation and then decide what they need to do with the numbers in order to solve the problem. In real life, we do this all the time. In this instance, the students were working backward: creating a story to go with a division problem. Amy has been very successful with this assignment. She is able to make up situations to match the equations, solve the problems, and also communicate her method of solving the problems. For the first problem she uses 7 circles to represent the 7 friends and then uses tally marks to divvy up the 42 balls. Her solution presents a clear picture of what division is about. You can also see that she is able to use standard division notation, including how to write about remainders. The math work this year will give Amy a chance to see how division relates to many different situations. (She'll also have a chance to think about what she might do with those remainders!) She's off to a good start.

APPENDIX 3.2
Helen's Portfolio

Dear Parents,

We have just completed a mathematics unit about division. The students have reviewed the work they completed. Attached is a sample of your child's work, chosen by your child to fit some of the categories listed below. Also, your child has written an explanation about why he or she chose to include each paper.

Categories for Portfolio Work
1. Best work
2. Favorite paper
3. A paper that describes a mathematical discovery or theory
4. A paper that clearly explains the student's thinking
5. A paper about an idea the student still wonders about or is unsure of

This portfolio is an example of the kind of assessment recommended nationally to evaluate children's learning and to communicate with parents. As you review the work with your child, some good questions for you to ask include: Why do you think that? Tell me more. Is there another way? Can you convince me your solution makes sense? How did you arrive at your answer? Why do you think your solution is reasonable? How did you use patterns to help you solve the problem?

Please comment about what you learned from your child and his/her work, what additional information you would like, and what your general reaction is to this kind of reporting about your child's learning. Also, feel free to include any questions you may have.

Sincerely,

Maryann Wickett

We think the concept is interesting, and helps us to understanding where her head is at and how her reasoning skills work. Helen seems to enjoy "explaining" anything — and this tapped right into that. She loved "explaining" it all to us.

Robin Smith

Divishion

~~Portfolio~~ Portfolio   Name Helen

Category # ① Title 20 ÷ 4   Date 2/12

It's my best work becaus
I'm proud of what I
did. I can see I've
improved by this Paper.
and It seems like
I understood it well

Category # ② Title The doorbell rings again Date 1/14

It's my favorite work
because I got to color,
and I was like doing
a sequal to the Dood
Bell rang.

Category # ④ Title 6 X 5 = 30   Date 2/28

I chose #4
because I showed all
the diffrent ways to get
6X5=30. The pictures
were easy to read, and
if not I put labels.

Name Helen   Date 3/13
Division Reflection

READING MY WORK

When I read my work, I felt suprised I knew
what I was doing, and
I had ecomplished so much.

I noticed that my work was
neet and complete, and
wasn't complete.

What surprised me was I knew what
I was doing, and understood
what I was doing.

What pleased me was that if I didn't
know what I was
doing, I would keep trying
and - made it

This is what I know about division:
I know how to explain my thinking correctly,
division and multipication are opesete but
do have some things in coinmon, how to make
sense of what I divide, and that you
can use just about anything you
want to divide, how to divide when
you can't cut it in half, How to play
Games with Divishion, how you can
also divide in groups.

How did you use patterns to help you learn about division?

By looking at what the
pattern does than apply it
to what even your dividing.

Helen   february 12.
and   Explain using words, Pictures
as you numbers in as many ways
as you can 20÷4

tally marks
||||| ||||| 10
||||| ||||| ||||| ||||| 20

5 groups of 4.

(tally groups in circles)

I think it's five because if you have 20 tally marks and you divide it among 4 children you'll get 5.

5   5
(|||||)   (|||||)

5   5
(|||||)   (|||||)

You can use circles and stars with division it's the same as leftovers. you just divide it in to equal groups.

Hannah had 20 spoons monica and her three sisters came, they had to divide 20÷4 how many did each get?
(5)

86   ▲ ▲ ▲

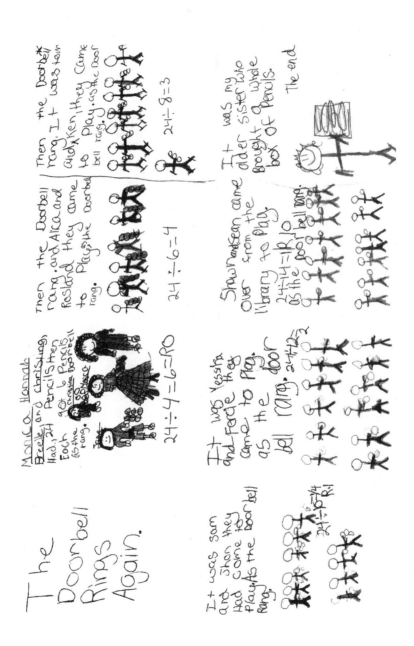

The
Doorbell
Rings
Again.

Monica Hannah
Breeke, and Chris Shag,
Had, 24 Pencils, then
Each the Doorbell rang.
got 6 Pencils
as the Chrissie Doorbell

$24 \div 4 = 6 = R0$

Then the Doorbell
rang, and Alka and
Rosland they came
to Play as the Doorbell
rang.

$24 \div 6 = 4$

Then the Doorbell
rang. It was teen
and Aiken they came
to Play as the Door
bell rang.

$24 \div 8 = 3$

It was Sam
and Shon they
Had come to
Play As the Doorbell
Rang.

$24 \div 6 = 4$
R:1

It was Yessha
and Farcie they
came to Play.
as the door
bell rang. $24 \div 12 = 2$

Shawn and Sean came
over from the
library to play
$24 \div 14 = 1R10$
as the door bell rang.

It was my
older sister who
brought a whole
box of Pencils.

The end

Helen   2/28

6X5

we have 30 kids in our class. we need to divide them into groups of five. How many groups? How many leftovers? Explain your soulution in as many ways as you can.

6X5=30

I need a 3.

The reason I should get this grade is because of all the ways I found and labels and Names of what it was, and easy to understand.

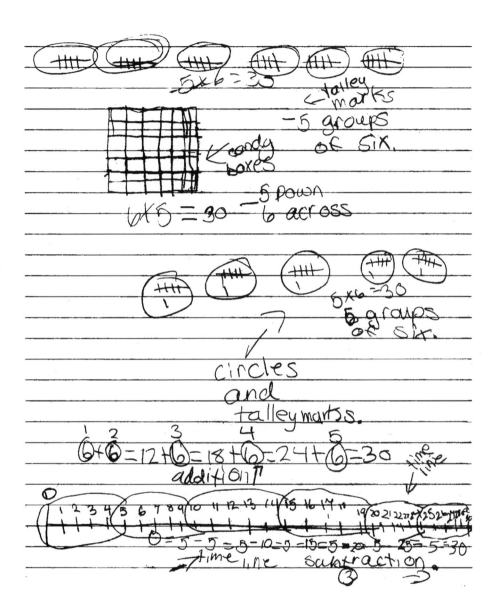

5×6 = 30

← talley marks

−5 groups of six.

← candy boxes

−5 down
6 across

6×5 = 30

5×6 = 30

5 groups of six.

circles and talleymarks.

1 2   3   4   5
6+6 = 12+6 = 18+6 = 24+6 = 30   time line
addition

0
0−5 −5 = 5−10−5 −15−5 = 20−5 −25−5 = 5−30
time line   subtraction.

Chapter 4
Homework

Homework is full of potential and peril. First, the potential: homework assignments can give parents a chance to observe and participate in the actual doing of math. When they play a game their child has taught them, parents become aware of the thinking inherent to the game. When they help collect data for an assignment, they see the connection between school math and the real world. When they see their child working out strategies for learning each of the addition facts, they see that memorization is not the only way to tackle learning basic skills.

At the same time, it's not unusual to hear, from two different sets of parents with children in the same class, that the school requires both too much homework and too little. And both sets of parents are probably right. Children and families have different needs, so one size does not fit all. Working out a useful and well-received homework program is tricky but ultimately worthwhile.

I'm lucky because I teach in a district that allows me a fair amount of flexibility. The district guidelines for first grade recommend that I assign occasional activities and projects that encourage parent-student interaction. And the guidelines continue to be similarly reasonable on up through the grades. Even as longer amounts of time are stipulated (forty-five minutes daily Monday through Thursday in fifth grade), the homework is expected to be an extension of class work and includes regular independent reading. Over the years I've tried to come up with a program that truly links school and home, serves as an extension of what we do in class, and doesn't overwhelm some children and make others long for more work to do.

As a first- and second-grade teacher, I send home only one assignment per week. At least half the time the assignment is math related. I make the assignment every Wednesday, and it goes home along with the official school newsletters, so parents know when to expect it. Completion of an assignment is always due the following Wednesday, so that there is plenty of time to work the activity into what is often a busy and demanding schedule. If I taught older children, I would send home a weekly *packet* of assignments that included at least one math assignment every week. However, I don't want my young students to become so overloaded with after-school activities (day care, special classes, and clubs, as well as homework) that they have no time just to be kids. Adults need to make sure that children have time to play alone or with friends, ride their bike, or curl up with a great book not because it's assigned but because reading is such a pleasure.

Still, I am an advocate of homework, even for young children, because it gives children a chance to extend what they've learned in school and gives parents a chance to see what school mathematics is all about. It's also an opportunity to emphasize that kids need to take responsibility for their own learning. This becomes increasingly important as students progress through the grades, but the foundation for being in charge can be laid early on. If children in the early grades have been responsible for explaining assignments to adults and carrying them out with adult help and encouragement, they're more likely to be able to do independent homework assignments in later grades.

Preparing Students to Be in Charge

One of my basic rules when I make a homework assignment is that my students must leave my classroom knowing what is expected of them and how to proceed. The assignment may involve teaching another family member to play a game, collecting data, or performing some kind of measurement, but I always do my best to make sure the children are prepared to do the work. This usually isn't terribly difficult, since the work I send home is an outgrowth of something we're doing in class. I just take a few moments to explain the assignment and answer any questions that come up. The payoff is that the student arrives home as the "expert" who can explain what the assignment is all about and in doing so has an opportunity to clarify and strengthen his or her own thinking. The parent is never put on the spot because he or she isn't a math whiz and is therefore unable to rescue the child from a confusing assignment. Instead, parent and child can enjoy the math together.

Newsletters That Introduce Homework

The newsletter below is one I might send home to introduce the start of a regular homework program. (This newsletter also introduces the idea of a homework diary, which I discuss later in this chapter.)

October 1

Dear Room 5 Families,

During back-to-school night, I mentioned that your child would soon be responsible for regular homework assignments. These assignments will give your child extra opportunities to do math and will also give you firsthand experience with our math program.

Expect an assignment every Wednesday, along with the school newsletter. It will be due the following Wednesday. Being responsible for a reasonable amount of homework can help your child grow as a student. To guide your child in assuming this new responsibility, take the time to talk through when he or she will do the task and who else needs to be involved. Your child should be the leader in this discussion but needs to know that you fully expect that the homework will get done sometime during the week.

The homework will almost always be an outgrowth of work we're doing at school. Your child should come home prepared to explain the assignment and knowledgeable about how to enlist the aid of family members. Please be respectful of the important role your child will assume in explaining the work to be done. If what he or she says is confusing, ask for clarification but try not to take over. I'll include notes that will help you and your child get the most out of each assignment. (Please keep any game rules that are part of the assignment. That way you can refer to the rules when you want to play the game later.)

I'm also asking that you give me important feedback by joining your child in filling out a "homework diary" at the conclusion of each assignment. (I'll send the diary home in a plastic sleeve. Please return it in the sleeve as well.) The diary keeps me informed and helps me make decisions about future assignments. I'd like both you and your child to indicate whether or not the assignment was enjoyable and what happened as you carried it out. It would also be helpful if you let me know whether the assignment was a good match for your child and if your child indicates what she or he learned from doing the assignment. If you have questions, include them in your comments. I'll send a written response the next time the diary comes home.

I'm looking forward to hearing from you and your child.

Cordially,

Nancy

The primary purpose of this letter is to let parents know how the homework program will work. A secondary purpose is to encourage them to join me in setting expectations by making sure the assignments are completed on time. I want parents to understand that they need to be firm about the overall expectation and yet guide their child to take responsibility for the many details of how the homework assignment gets done.

The process usually works well. However, a few parents invariably mention that conflicts have arisen over homework, usually because it has been put off until the last minute. I encourage these parents to talk with their child about homework when everyone is relaxed and to say something like this: *Last week, getting your homework done was a problem. That wasn't any fun, and you didn't learn much from the assignment. Let's look at the calendar and pick a time we can set aside to do this week's homework. I want you to help choose the time so that you can be in charge.* This approach often seems to help, especially the notion that it's possible to anticipate a problem and prevent it from happening by talking things through beforehand. I explain that the an-ounce-of-prevention-is-worth-a-pound-of-cure maxim is central in helping the classroom run smoothly and that it can work for families, too. I reinforce this idea in class by reminding the children on Monday that their homework is due in two days.

A Homework Diary

I've been experimenting with a homework diary as a way for parents and children to give feedback about how each assignment worked out. The diary has a threefold purpose:

1. It gives me feedback about how assignments are being received and carried out at home. (This is especially helpful when the assignment is to play a game and there is no written work that needs to be returned.)

2. It encourages positive involvement and reflection on the part of the parent and child.

3. Asking parents to be part of an ongoing reporting process is another way of telling them they are an important part of the learning process.

The diary consists of half sheets of 8½-by-11-inch paper stapled together between construction paper covers. The first sheet (see Figure 4.1) reminds parents about the kinds of information I'm looking for. The remaining sheets look like the one in Figure 4.2.

I send the diary and homework assignment home in a plastic sleeve, along with a reminder that the diary and plastic sleeve need to be returned, as well as any written work required by the assignment. (If the assignment is to play a game several times, I make it

Homework Diary

Please fill out a page in this homework diary each time it comes home with an assignment.

I'd like to hear from both **parents** and **students** if the assignment was enjoyable and what happened as you did the assignment. **Parents** should also let me know if the assignment was a good match for your child. **Students** should let me know what you learned from doing the assignment.

If you have any questions, please include them in your comments. I'll respond, and you'll be able to read my comments the next time the diary comes home.

Thanks for your feedback.

FIGURE 4.1.▲ The homework diary instruction page.

Name _____

Homework Activity _____

Participants _____

Comments:

FIGURE 4.2.▲ The homework diary entry form.

clear that the game rules should remain at home for future reference. I often include a manila envelope or folder with the first set of game rules so that families have a place to store them.)

Below are some of the comments I got from first graders and their parents after an assignment in which I asked them to play two games (Counters in a Cup and On and Off) that involve breaking numbers into two parts:

Jill: This was fun.

Mom: Jill was very adept at these games and seemed to enjoy them a lot. It seems this is a great way to get comfortable with adding and subtracting.

Mom: Mandy became more proficient at counting and figuring the answer in her head as the games progressed. It was interesting to see how her proficiency improved. She enjoyed this, and I think it's an excellent way to visualize math problems.

Sally: I liked playing Counters in a Cup and On and Off.

Mom: I watched Sally play On and Off, and she explained how it worked. She showed me how all the different combinations added up to the same number each time. Then I played On and Off with the number 15. Then we played Counters in a Cup. When Sally had her turn she would sometimes group the "out" counters in 2s or 3s to make it easier for me to count. One time the counters didn't add up to the proper number, and we were puzzled. But then we found one counter under Sally's knee—and it added up correctly then!

Luna: I found out that it was fun figuring out numbers.

Dad: At first, Luna was counting out to figure out the answer. After a couple of turns she began to recognize the combinations.

Geoff: It was fun.

Mom: We played with marshmallows, which was wild because we had never, ever thrown a marshmallow before! The assignment seemed very well suited to Geoff's math skills! Thank you.

I find myself smiling and feeling much more connected to what goes on at home when I read these statements. They tell me that the games I'm sending home are appropriate for my students and that the assignments are letting parents know about my math program. It's a great pleasure to know that parents notice their children's growth and understand the goals of the assignments.

It's also important to know when a child is not enthusiastic about an assignment:

> Alan: I liked it but I wish you didn't send as much Counters in a Cup home.
>
> Mom: Alan became frustrated and maybe bored at the Counters in a Cup game, perhaps because there were quite a few [grids to fill in] and it was easy for him. It was difficult to get him to finish the whole assignment.

How can I best help Alan and his parents have a more positive experience with homework? I can start by suggesting that Alan play the games with larger numbers, letting his parents know it's okay to adapt assignments so they will challenge him more. I also know that Alan sometimes needs extra adult encouragement in class to do assignments that are *not* easy for him. Perhaps there is a pattern here that goes beyond the particular assignment. The homework diary helps me sort out these issues and deal with them more effectively.

Because I don't want the diary to become an unwieldy burden, I make a point of not promising to respond to every entry. But I frequently include comments in newsletters about how much I'm enjoying reading the diaries, and I'll sometimes write short comments in a particular diary. I've also used the diary to send longer personal notes to some families. For instance, with a number game that can be played using a range of numbers, I may tell some families that their child might benefit most by using a fairly small number of counters to start with. Other families get a handwritten message saying their child is ready to work with larger numbers. The diary is a low-key way to communicate to parents about the ever-changing needs of their child, particularly when I feel a little extra attention might help a child with a concept we're studying but I don't want to suggest there are major problems that need to be addressed. It also enables me to let parents of particularly capable students know that I notice how well their children are doing and that I'm adjusting the curriculum accordingly.

Helping Parents Be More Prepared

One of the things I've been working on lately is offering suggestions to parents so that they're better prepared to work with their children in a positive way. One of the perils of homework is that parent and child may tangle over how to accomplish a task and end up in an unproductive clash of wills.

Now when I send home an assignment, I usually include a note suggesting ways parents can ask helpful questions or share their own strategies and at the same time respect their child's way of doing things. I hope these suggestions not only prevent unnecessary stalemates, but also encourage everyone to think more deeply about the mathematics involved.

Appendix 4.1 contains some examples of my homework assignments, along with the related notes to parents. The assignments themselves are not important; often I attach a cover sheet to instructions that have been provided as a blackline master in a teacher resource. What is important is the issue or issues the note addresses: encouraging parents to model strategies in open-ended ways, offering a rationale for playing the same game many times, etc.

Following Up

Once a homework assignment is returned to school and placed in the child's math folder (or tucked into a large pocket affixed to the wall), I try to follow up in a more significant way than simply checking off who has and has not turned in the assignment.

Sometimes I design a classroom activity that uses data collected by the children. Sometimes I ask the students to share with their classmates the new strategies they developed when they played an assigned game at home. Sometimes we just have a brief class discussion about how the assignment went. Whatever the particular means, by doing some sort of follow-up I strengthen the tie between home and school and give the children an additional reason for doing their best on homework assignments. And whenever a homework diary entry includes questions, I make sure to respond immediately, also in the diary.

Occasionally a teacher needs to take remedial action with regard to homework. My friend Carrie Oretsky was less than happy with the quality of the homework assignments that her fifth graders were returning to school. Carrie sends home a weekly homework packet every Monday. The packet includes at least one mathematical problem, with the instruction that students are to write about and/or draw their solution, not just give the answer. At the beginning of the school year Carrie found that very few of her students were explaining their solutions. Without an explanation, she had no way of knowing how a student's thinking had gone wrong when a solution was incorrect and no way to confirm that a child really understood the assignment even when the answer was correct.

Reminding her students that they were supposed to show their thinking didn't seem to improve the quality of the work coming in. So Carrie took a tack that would give her students a better understanding of what she expected, encourage self-assessment, and let parents see the importance of involving students in setting standards. She began by saying, "Let's talk about what a wonderful homework paper would look like." Then she explained that the class would develop a five-point rubric that they would then use to grade their homework. After she and the children had engaged in some spirited discussion, she listed their final ideas on the board:

▲ Shows excellent effort.
▲ Shows lots of detail.

▲ Shows evidence of revision.

▲ Explains thinking.

▲ Is legible.

▲ Shows risk taking.

Carrie explained that a paper with all these characteristics would be assigned a rating of 5. The class went on to describe an average paper, one that would qualify as a 3 on the scale, then did the same thing for papers that would receive a 1, a 2, and a 4. Here's the rest of the rubric, which Carrie's class now uses to grade homework assignments.

A paper deserving a score of 4:

▲ Lists strategies with no explanations.

▲ Shows evidence of some revision.

▲ Shows extra effort.

▲ Is correct.

▲ Is complete.

A paper deserving a score of 3:

▲ Shows an answer only, with no explanation.

▲ Shows no evidence of revision.

▲ Shows no evidence of extra effort.

▲ Is correct but without extra details.

A paper deserving a score of 2:

▲ Is incorrect.

▲ Shows hardly any effort.

▲ May be messy or hard to read.

A paper deserving a score of 1:

▲ Has no name.

▲ Shows no effort.

▲ Is incorrect.

▲ Is incomplete.

▲ Is illegible.

▲ Is not turned in, with an excuse like "My dog ate it."

Carrie says that having this rubric has made "a huge difference" in the quality of homework that the children are now bringing in. Participating in creating the rubric has helped her students internalize the high standards she expects of them and given them a road map to follow when doing their work. The quality of the ideas generated by the children tells me that Carrie's students had heard what she was asking for earlier in the year; being given the responsibility of creating the rubric encouraged them to begin to act on her earlier suggestions.

Now, on Fridays, when the homework packet is due, students come into the room and place their assignments in their individual homework folder. They grade their own paper using the rubric as a guide and then exchange papers with a peer, who records a second grade. Carrie collects the folders and later records a third rating, the one she thinks the paper merits. (Figure 4.3 is the form Carrie uses to record these ratings for each student over a semester's time.)

Carrie says there is rarely a significant difference between her grade and those of the students. If there is, her grade prevails and she makes a point of discussing the difference with the child. This disparity in thinking alerts Carrie to those few children who still need help assessing their own work. Being able to assess one's work realistically is crucial both in school and in the workplace. The work that Carrie's students do when they reflect on the quality of their assignment is as important as doing the assignment in the first place.

During parent conferences, Carrie shares the homework evaluations with each student's parents. They look at the student's homework folder and talk about how the homework rubric was developed. Carrie uses these discussions to make the point that students need to learn to assess their own work and to *internalize* the high standards we have for them. Parents see the value of getting children involved in assessment and the importance of having classroom teachers who encourage students to set high standards for themselves. They are also able to take a more informed interest in their child's homework assignments.

Date	You	A Peer	Teacher	Date	You	A Peer	Teacher
M				M			
TU				TU			
W				W			
M				M			
TU				TU			
W				W			
M				M			
TU				TU			
W				W			
M				M			
TU				TU			
W				W			
M				M			
TU				TU			
W				W			
M				M			
TU				TU			
W				W			
M				M			
TU				TU			
W				W			

FIGURE 4.3.▲ Homework rating sheet.

Homework in the Upper Grades

Upper-grade students also benefit from doing homework assignments that are an outgrowth of school and that involve their families. Here's an assignment given to a group of fourth graders by their teacher, Annette Raphael (for some background on how Annette prepared the children for this assignment and how the assignment became the basis for a math night with parents, see Chapter 6):

> Today in class we estimated different things, including height, length, time, amounts, and weight. For next Tuesday I would like you to do a personal estimation project. Choose something that would be fun to estimate. My ideas, which are seldom as interesting or as inventive as yours, include:
>
> ▲ The number of grapes in a bunch.
> ▲ How many times the refrigerator door opens in 24 hours at your house.
> ▲ How many grocery items end up in your cart when you go shopping.
> ▲ How many cars pass by your house in a fifteen-minute period.
> ▲ How many windows (or electrical outlets or stairs) there are in your house.
> ▲ How many words (or letters) there are in a paragraph in the newspaper.
> ▲ How many children in the lower school have a birthday in March.
>
> Write down your estimate before you actually gather the data. *This is very important.* Then gather the data to find out what the actual number or measurement is. The final step is the most interesting to me. In writing, I would like you to tell me why you chose the thing you did to estimate, your strategy for making the estimate, what you did to gather the information to check your estimate, and whether your estimate turned out to be a good one. You might also think about whether the answer would likely be more-or-less the same or very different if you did the same activity again. (For example: Does the refrigerator door open more frequently on weekends than on weekdays? Would counting your windows in the middle of the night yield a different result? Can the number of grapes in one bunch be a lot different from the number in another bunch?)
>
> Extra: On a sheet of drawing paper, make a representation of what you estimated, let me know the actual amount in some way, and write one sentence telling me something interesting about this project.

Notice the way Annette personalized the assignment, explaining that she was interested in having them expand on their choices and strategies. The last few sentences are especially important, because they tell her students that she's interested in their thinking, not just their data.

This assignment gave Annette's students an opportunity to gather and analyze data, an important part of any statistics unit. It also gave the families of her students a chance to see how thought-provoking and relevant a school mathematics program can be.

Conclusion

Homework can be a critical link between home and school. To make it a positive one, I try to:

1. Communicate clearly with parents about the purpose of the homework program and each person's role in making the program successful.

2. Send home assignments that are an extension of classroom learning, make sense to children, and sometimes involve other family members.

3. Prepare parents so that they can support their child and even have fun being involved in mathematics.

4. Ask families to give feedback about homework.

5. Follow up on homework assignments in the classroom.

6. Be clear, with both students and their parents, about my expectations.

Whenever I follow these steps, I come closer to my goal of using homework to expand learning for children, their parents, and me.

APPENDIX 4.1
Examples of Primary-Grade Homework Assignments, With
Accompanying Notes to Parents

Name _____

Math Homework
Comparison Games*
Due Next Wednesday

Assignment: Teach someone in your family to play Compare and/or Double Compare. Play the game(s) several times during the next week.

How to Play Compare: Deal a deck of number cards (which is included separately) equally between two players. Each player turns over the top card of her or his stack, and the players then mentally compare the two cards. The person who has the larger number says "More." Play proceeds in this way, each person turning over her or his next card and comparing the two quantities. No cards are taken; there is no winner or loser.

How to Play Double Compare: This game works the same way except each player turns over two cards and the sums of each player's cards are compared.

Note to Parents: Help your child find a safe place to store the cards and the game instructions. (You can keep these and other game instructions that will be coming home later in the year in the attached manila envelope. The cards will be used for several future homework assignments this year and next.)

The instructions for the games are included, but let your child decide which game to play and explain how to play it. You can encourage your child to think and reason by asking questions like *How do you know who has more?* while you play the game. Make sure you do this with a light touch. Expect a lot of counting—careful counting is one of the main objectives of these games.

You can also do some thinking out loud about your reasoning. You might say something like, *Hmm, I've got a 5 and a 5. You've got a 9 and a 3; 5 plus 5 equals 10 for me, but you've got even more than 10. I know that because 9 plus one more makes 10, but you've got 3 extras.* Most important: make sure you respect your child's current reasoning.

*These comparison games are a version of the game War, included in the first-grade curriculum of TERC's Investigations in Number, Data, and Space series, published by Dale Seymour.

Name _____

Math Homework
Counters in a Cup and On and Off*
Diary Due Next Wednesday

Assignment: Play the games Counters in a Cup and On and Off several times at home this next week. Write about your experiences in your Homework Diary. I love hearing about your experiences doing homework with your family.

How to Play Counters in a Cup: Counters in a Cup is a partner game that requires a quantity of counters from 5 to 10. After the quantity has been established, one person hides some of the counters in the cup; the other partner has to figure out how many are hidden based on the number that are left outside the cup. The numbers of counters in and out of the cup are recorded on a grid. Several rounds of hiding and recording using the same total quantity completes the game.

How to Play On and Off: On and Off is played by choosing a quantity of counters and tossing the counters above a piece of paper. A record is made of the number that lands on the paper as well as the number that lands off. One game consists of several rounds using the same quantity.

Note to Parents: Your child has learned the rules of these games in class. Now that the rules have been mastered, he or she can focus on the mathematical content of the games. Make sure you save the game rules so you can play these games again in the future. The more often students play these games, the more opportunities they have to practice math skills, to think and reason mathematically, and to reinforce the mathematical ideas we're introducing in class. I encourage you to continue playing these games—and any others I assign as homework—many times in the weeks ahead. They will help your child become knowledgeable about number combinations through frequent experience rather than by rote memorization. When you play the two new games, let your child decide how many counters to use. As you observe your child playing the games, you can adjust the level of challenge for your child by suggesting a larger or smaller number of counters. We also hope you'll have fun!

*These games are also from TERC's first-grade Investigations series.

Name _____

Math Homework
Strategies for Single-Digit Addition Facts*
Due Next Wednesday

Assignment: Make sure you know your doubles. If you don't, practice them every day.

1 + 1   2 + 2   3 + 3   4 + 4   5 + 5   6 + 6   7 + 7   8 + 8   9 + 9   10 + 10

In class we looked at the chart for the addition facts from 0 + 0 through 10 + 10. There were 121 facts—phew!! That's a lot. When we looked at the chart closely, we discovered that there were many facts that everyone already knew, so we crossed those out. The facts listed below are ones that you may still need to practice.

4 + 3	5 + 3	6 + 3	7 + 3	8 + 3	9 + 3
	5 + 4	6 + 4	7 + 4	8 + 4	9 + 4
		6 + 5	7 + 5	8 + 5	9 + 5
			7 + 6	8 + 6	9 + 6
				8 + 7	9 + 7
					9 + 8

The important thing is to have *strategies* that make sense to you so you can quickly find the answers when you need them. Each day, choose three or more of these additions facts. On a separate sheet of paper, write down your *strategies* for getting the answer to each fact.

Note to Parents: The purpose of this assignment is to encourage the children to use their number sense (especially the ability to decompose numbers and knowledge about how numbers relate to one another) to develop strategies for efficiently doing single-digit addition. Different children may come up with different strategies to solve the same problem—the important thing is for each child to think about what works for him or her. Memorization is less important than having a quick and accurate way of coming up with the answer. For instance, when I want the answer to 8 + 9, I say to myself, 8 + 8 = 16 so 8 + 9 = 17. I can do this in the blink of an eye. In class we're talking about the kinds of strategies that make us mathematically powerful, so your child will have many ideas to draw from. You might want to share some of your strategies with your child. Just remember that your child may go about solving the problems differently and that's fine. We must each construct understanding that works for us.

*The assignment grew out of our work based on the Math By All Means unit *Probability, Grades 1–2,* although this was not one of the homework assignments listed in the unit.

Chapter 5
Classroom Volunteers

I was surprised many years ago when a parent said that she liked volunteering in the classroom because she came away from the experience with ideas about how to interact with her daughter. It had never occurred to me that my everyday talk with children could serve as a useful model to parents. But it's true that an observant parent can gain helpful insights by watching a teacher communicate with her or his students. As kindergarten teacher Ann Carlyle says, "Parents who are in the classroom learn how the teacher poses questions and challenges to children to get their cooperation."

When parents spend time in the classroom during a math period, they're able to observe in action ideas and strategies that have been discussed in newsletters and other forms of school-home communication. Parents also learn from interacting with a whole classroom of children. They see how different children approach the same problem and often end up learning something about their own child's uniqueness.

Knowing that parents are listening carefully can be anxiety-provoking to a teacher, especially at first. It's hard not to feel tense knowing that another person is probably judging your performance in some way. But the feeling is natural: almost every teacher has experienced it at one time or another. Like anything else, it does get easier to be under the watchful eyes of visitors if it happens regularly enough. It's also comforting to remember that most parents really do want to be helpful and do see their child's teacher as a person with valuable skills, knowledge, and wisdom.

The Changing Times

There was a time when I had a parent volunteer in my classroom almost every day. With changes in the economy, work force, and family structure, those days are over, at least in the community in which I teach. Parents have less time to devote to volunteering in the classroom and can't come in as frequently as they once did. This was brought home to me when my volunteers began not showing up when they were supposed to. After a few years of frustration at not being able to do things I'd planned when they didn't show up, I realized that I had to make some changes in my expectations.

At the same time, the way I structure my classroom has changed. I no longer need volunteers to run learning stations every day, because I do more whole-class instruction. Nowadays, my students frequently work alone or in pairs to solve problems, play math games, or explore a mathematical idea after being introduced to the activity as a whole group. Then, once the children have had a chance to work on the activity, we come back together as a group to share solutions or strategies. True, parent volunteers can still play a role in this context by observing and maybe being a child's partner when a game is being played. But I want my parent volunteers to get more involved in our mathematics program, especially in first grade.

My colleague Lianne Morrison suggested a model I like: it enables parents to become more knowledgeable about the classroom mathematics program without requiring a regular time commitment throughout the year.

It works like this. Twice a year, I go back to my old learning-center structure for mathematics instruction. In first grade I schedule centers in the fall, when the children are exploring patterns, and then again later in the year, during our geometry unit. (I choose these two particular units because when I teach them I like to be free to work with a small group of students.) Each unit runs for three or four weeks, four days a week. For the duration of the unit I divide the class into four groups. Each group rotates through four centers during each week of the unit. I teach at one of the centers, my aide teaches at another, and parent volunteers teach at one or two of the remaining centers. (Some years I have a student teacher, and sometimes I set up an independent center if I don't have two volunteers available for each time slot.)

Scheduling Volunteers

A few weeks before the centers are to begin, I put an announcement like this in a newsletter:

During much of October, the class will be engaged in a mathematical exploration of pattern. If you can volunteer to work with a small group of children for one hour on any of the dates listed on the form below, circle the time(s) you are available. *Please return this form no later than Thursday, September 25.* I'll let you know the date(s) you are scheduled to volunteer in the classroom by Wednesday, October 1. When you arrive in the classroom, I'll explain what you and your group of students will be doing. Thanks for your help!

Monday	Tuesday	Wednesday	Thursday
Oct. 6, 11:00	Oct. 7, 10:30	Oct. 8, 10:30	Oct. 9, 10:30
Oct. 13, 11:00	Oct. 14, 10:30	Oct. 15, 10:30	Oct. 16, 10:30
Oct. 20, 11:00	Oct. 21, 10:30	Oct. 22, 10:30	Oct. 23, 10:30

Your name _____   Your child's name _____

After the deadline for signing up has passed, I set up a schedule and let each volunteer know when I'm expecting him or her to help out in the classroom. I've found that the parents who volunteer under these circumstances are committed and rarely forget to come.

Setting Up the Centers

Being well organized in general, as well as being specific about what each volunteer is expected to do, makes it more likely that using parent volunteers will be a successful experience for everyone involved. I schedule the parent to arrive at least ten minutes before the center period begins, so that he or she has time to read the plan and ask questions before diving in. (The children are either at recess or doing silent reading while I talk to the parent.) If I have a math resource book that describes the activity a parent is in charge of, I copy the appropriate pages or give the parent the book. Otherwise, I make up my own set of instructions. Sometimes the instructional plan I write up is fairly detailed, describing what the children will be doing and offering suggestions about how to interact with the group of students. I let the parent read through the plan uninterrupted, and then make sure I'm around to answer questions.

Then I spend a few minutes talking about the materials the children will be using, discussing cleanup, showing how the parent center activity relates to the other parts of the unit, and/or explaining the underlying mathematics involved in the activity. For instance, during the geometry unit, when I ask parents to work with children who are filling in blackline shapes with pattern blocks, I might say: *This activity gives the children lots of practice solving spatial problems. Part of understanding geometry is seeing how geometric shapes can be broken down into other geometric figures. The children will be encountering this same big idea with me at the quilt block center.*

An Example of a Volunteer Lesson Plan

Here's an example of a lesson plan I might give to a parent during a geometry unit with first graders:

Pattern Block Center
During this activity the children will be covering animal shapes with pattern blocks and counting the number of blocks needed to do so.

After they've gotten some experience with this procedure and have a feel for how many blocks it takes to cover a shape, they'll be asked to make an estimate of how many blocks they'll need to cover their next animal shape and record their estimate. Part of your job will be to familiarize the children with this procedure and with the recording form.

1. Explain to the children that they will be using the pattern blocks to cover up the large animal shapes on the cards and then counting the number of blocks they used.

2. Let each child choose an animal, make a verbal estimate of how many blocks might be needed, and begin working.

3. As children finish covering the shapes, remind them to count the number of blocks they actually used.

4. When you're sure everyone has had a chance to cover at least one animal shape, ask the children to stop working for a moment. Show them the form they'll be using to record their estimate, the actual count, and the difference between the two numbers. You might model this whole procedure by going through the process yourself with one of the animal shapes, doing the estimating, covering, and counting.

5. Ask the children to write their names and the date on their recording sheets and let them get back to work.

6. Circulate among the children, observing how they go about the task. This activity is likely to come easily for some children and be more difficult for others. To someone ready for a challenge you might say: *I noticed that you estimated 10 blocks to cover your shape. You came close to your estimate by using 12 blocks. What blocks could you change to get even closer to your estimate?* Or: *What's the fewest number of blocks that you can use to cover the shape?* Others may be experiencing some frustrations and may need help in focusing on the lines. It's okay to suggest that a child begin working by placing a block on one side of the animal shape, but try not to take over. Sometimes simply saying, *What shape will you try next?* provides support and gives the child motivation to keep trying.

7. When I ring the bell for cleanup, please collect the children's papers and remind them to put the blocks back in the containers before coming to sit quietly on the rug.

Thanks so much for helping out today.

While writing plans for parents to follow, I mentally picture what I might do if I were teaching the lesson and think through how the children might respond. I know I can't anticipate everything that will come up, but I hope that if I give a few examples, parents will have a clearer picture of how to proceed. Writing up these plans is time-consuming, but the payoff is seeing parents fit comfortably into their roles as volunteers. These plans get filed carefully, ready to be used the next time I teach the same unit.

Getting Feedback

At the end of the period, especially if the children have gone out to recess, I try to spend a few minutes debriefing the parent volunteer. I ask how things went in general and if anything noteworthy happened. I might even ask her or him to jot down a few notes that might be helpful either in making the center run more smoothly in the future or in reminding me of something mathematically significant that happened. I answer any questions the volunteer has, once again trying to make links between what happened in the center and the general goals of the mathematics unit.

I find that parents generally enjoy this opportunity to be a meaningful part of the classroom; they go home feeling satisfied that a coherent and important unit of study is unfolding. I'm not stressed, because I haven't been stage center for any length of time. Instead, I've enjoyed the opportunity to work with a small group of children knowing that all my students have been appropriately occupied.

A Kindergarten Volunteer Program

Ann Carlyle, who teaches kindergarten, sees working with parents as an integral part of her job. I asked Ann to describe her experience working with parents as classroom volunteers: "All in all, I see my role as an early childhood teacher as also being a teacher to the parents of my kids. I only have these kids for a year. Their parents will be working with them for the next twelve years and longer. So the time I spend thinking about how to make my expectations and their responsibilities more clear is worth it."

She uses parent volunteers regularly in her classroom. "I have some parents who volunteer for a half hour to an hour every week or every other week. There are a few who drop in when they get a chance. I never know when, but I try to take advantage of their time with us. But I too have seen less and less participation as more and more parents have needed to work for actual wages in the past five years.

"Thinking about what motivates each volunteer helps me find the right kind of experience for them in the room. When parents volunteer they want to see how school is going for their own child. They want to get a sense of the program and of how I interact with children. They want to make sure that their child is okay. They want to see how the other kids in the class stack up and where their child fits in the scheme of things. For these reasons, I usually set up a small-group activity that all or most of the children rotate through. The activity usually involves physical skills like cutting, pasting, and following directions, and there is almost always a product of some kind, a visible proof of all the work the parent did to assist us in the classroom.

"I try to arrange for parents to be in the classroom when there is lots of activity and movement. I want them to see how independent and purposeful the children are. The project and the materials are set out on a table in an organized way. There is a roster of the students in the class. (My kids love to find their name and cross it off when they do these tasks.) I select the first group to go to the parent table, making sure that the group has some children who will require little assistance and some who will require more. Usually the child of the volunteering parent wants to be a part of the first group. Some children finish the tasks more quickly than others; whenever someone is done, another student comes in and starts work. That way, there is a great deal of productivity at that table. Usually I have the children display their project as soon as they finish. At the end of the session, I thank the parent helper and mention that we couldn't do this kind of work without his or her help.

"While I've got them there, I model how to work with children who are having trouble, how to support children who need encouragement. I also chat with the parents (sort of over the heads of the children) about the interesting variety of responses: Jason is something of a minimalist, Moses loves to use glue, Chris almost always tries to make her project look exactly like the sample, Tessa is so creative with her embellishments. Comments like this show the parent that I expect different levels of response and am aware of the different levels of skill and alternative approaches. I have to be sensitive about not sharing too much personal information about children and their abilities but enough to allow the parent to work with the child.

"I try to pick and choose the tasks I ask parents to do. I rarely ask them to do boring work like running off copies in the office. When parents help at school, I try to keep them in the class so they can see what is going on. I do ask my parents who are non-English speakers to help at home by cutting out paper shapes, etc. They want to volunteer, but don't know how they can help. I encourage those parents who are more aware of the stages of child development and the methods of language acquisition to go shopping in our class shoe store, bake pretend cookies in our home center, things like that. The children see that parents can play with them in a way that is noncontrolling. These play situations usually come *after* the product-oriented project that I have asked them to supervise."

Ann is able to use her volunteers so effectively and spend so much time interacting with them because early in the year she places a high premium on teaching her kids to work independently. The ebb and flow of children at the volunteer table works well because when students finish their project, they know how to move on to a self-selected project in the block corner, the class store, the home center. What a terrific environment for parents who are hungry for models that will help them raise capable, responsible children.

A Second-Grade Volunteer

Rusty Bresser has the good luck to have a loyal volunteer who comes to his class every week. She knows the routine of the class, so her presence enables Rusty to teach more effectively. She helps individual students and gets a real taste of the second-grade math program. Here's what Rusty has to say.

"In my second-grade class, I have one parent, Stacy, who comes in every Tuesday morning for about an hour and a half. I use her in two ways. When the kids first come in, they have a warm-up that they do. During this part of the period, I have Stacy work with two students who have lots of problems with mathematics. Her assistance gives them the boost they need. Without her, I'd have to be there to support them. This frees me up to assist more children and to check their homework.

"Later in the period, when the class is playing a math game or solving a problem, I have Stacy be someone's partner. I always team her up with a different student, so that everyone gets a chance to work with her. Stacy is exposed to the range of thinkers in the class, and she definitely has an appreciation for my job. She's an interested, involved parent in the community and I'm sure she spreads the word in terms of the kind of mathematics she sees going on in the classroom."

Conclusion

When I look at these different ways of using parent volunteers, I see they all have certain things in common. Perhaps most important to the success of a volunteer program, the teacher has to put thought into what the volunteers will be doing and find a way to communicate those plans and expectations. This can be accomplished through a written plan, by making sure there's time to talk with the volunteers, or by setting up an activity that the volunteer does regularly. In all of these models, parents learn more about the mathematics program in general and about their child in particular; they may even become a goodwill ambassador to the community.

Chapter 6
Family Math Nights

One of the best ways to inform parents about mathematics reform is to invite them to a problem-solving session (or series of sessions) with their child. The Family Math program, which was developed by the Equals staff at the University of California's Lawrence Hall of Science, is an inspiring source of activities and organizational ideas. The introduction to the book *Family Math* (Stenmark et al. 1986) poses the question, "Who teaches Family Math?" The answer: "Anyone who is enthusiastic, kind, and not afraid." Personally, I'd have to delete the phrase "not afraid," because I remember being plenty afraid as I prepared my classroom for my first family math night. I also remember the tremendous high I felt about halfway through that first session when I realized how capable the students sounded as they shared their strategies for playing the game Target Addition. I wasn't the only one impressed. Parents were delighted to hear their children articulating problem-solving strategies in an environment that encouraged them to take intellectual risks. This experience was pivotal in helping some parents understand and appreciate a problem-solving approach to mathematics.

According to the introduction to *Family Math*, the program was developed because teachers "told us that parents were frustrated in not knowing enough about their children's math program to help them." Holding a family math night does more than just pass along knowledge about math content. It helps create a mathematical community that includes parents, children, and educators; it offers the potential for everyone involved to learn that doing math can be fun and accessible to anyone who is willing to work at it; it brings home the notion that the best way to learn something is to do it; and it can even help those who have never before been successful in math experience the delight and power that comes from sticking with a task and mastering it.

The best way to learn more about organizing a family math night is to use the resources developed by the Equals staff. These include *Family Math* and *Family Math for Young Children*, a new book about working with students who are from four to eight years old. Workshops designed for teachers, parents, or anyone else interested in doing family math are scheduled at various sites throughout the country. You can learn more about these resources by calling the Family Math program at the Lawrence Hall of Science in Berkeley, California. (See the resources bibliography for details.)

What Does Family Math Night Look Like?

Family Math makes the point that there's no one way to implement a family math program. I knew there would be high interest among the parents of the two second-grade classes at my school the first time I offered a family math night, so I included only second-grade families and limited the number of participants to the number of chairs my classroom could comfortably accommodate. Next door, my colleague Suzanne Latham was conducting a first-grade session for the families of the two first-grade classes. Other teachers have conducted mixed-grade sessions. The important thing is to think through what works in your situation and with your resources.

For my first time I used the generic lesson plan at the back of *Family Math*, focusing the evening's activities on the mathematical strand of number. I drew confidence from the fact that this format had been successful for many others in the past. I tailored the generic lesson plan to my situation by choosing activities from the book and from other sources that seemed a good match for my particular group of children. The generic schedule unfolds like this:

▲ Openers
▲ Introductions
▲ Math activities
▲ Homework assignment
▲ Comments and evaluations

As people finished filling out their nametags at my first family math night, I invited them to play one of the simple number games that were described on large posters placed around the room. These "openers" were self-explanatory and designed to give participants something mathematical to do while we waited for everyone to arrive.

Then I called the group together for introductions. We talked briefly about the number games they'd just finished playing, and I explained the first activity of the night, Double-Digit Cover-Up (see Figure 6.1). I chose this game, which is a variation of the Double-Digit activity in *Family Math*, because it provides opportunities for learners to develop an understanding of our number system and I felt it would be accessible to second graders. The variation has the advantage of using simple-to-make concrete materials. (In preparation, a parent volunteer and I duplicated extra copies of the grid on heavy card stock, then cut some into individual squares and some into ten-square strips.) To play the basic game, each player needs a grid to cover. For the cooperative variation, only one grid is needed.

As part of my introduction to the game I had the children figure out how many squares were in the grid. Then families played the game. After about ten minutes, I called the group back together for a brief "where's the math?" discussion. I wanted to make sure that we spent a few moments reflecting on the kind of mathematical thinking and practice the children were getting from playing the game before going on. We talked about how the simple manipulatives created a concrete model for what a hundred looks like. Parents liked the game, and made meaningful comments.

▲ "Since there were only seven rolls of the die, we had to make careful decisions after our last few rolls."

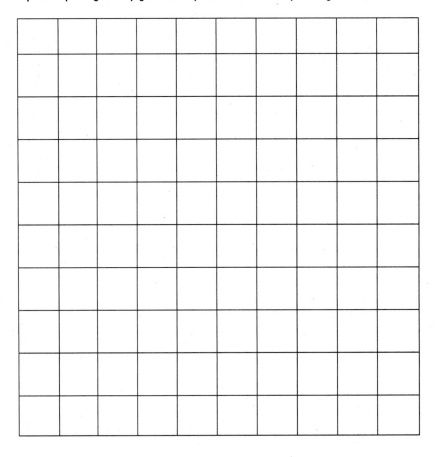

Double Digit Cover-Up

Rules

- Players take turns rolling the die. All players use the same roll of the die.
- Each player takes as many single squares or ten-strips as the number on the die and places them on her or his 100-grid.
- The die is rolled exactly seven times. Players must take either squares or strips on each of the seven rolls. A player *may not* take both squares *and* strips on the same roll.
- The object of the game is to cover the grid without going over. Each square covered on the grid counts as one point.

Cooperative Variation

- All players work together to cover one grid. Players keep a record of their scores to see if they are improving as they get more experience and develop strategies.

FIGURE 6.1.▲ A family math night activity.

▲ "I liked that you could figure up the score mentally or use the manipulatives to keep track. This gave everyone in our family a chance to participate."

▲ "I think this game gives practice with estimation and really helps kids think about larger numbers."

▲ "This is a fun way to do math."

Throughout the evening I continued this pattern of introducing an activity, providing time to play the game, and then discussing the game as a group. I taught a total of three games: Double-Digit Cover-Up (discussed above); Target Math (from *Family Math*); and the Adding and Subtracting Game, which was created by Aaron and Caleb, two of my second graders. (Including Aaron and Caleb's game gave me a chance to talk about how my students had explored the idea of fair games during our unit on probability.) The rules for the Adding and Subtracting Game are shown in Figure 6.2. I have edited the spelling, but the words are Aaron and Caleb's.

I ended the evening with a homework assignment, which was to continue playing the three games we had learned. Families

---

The Adding and Subtracting Game
by Aaron and Caleb

You need: 2 dice and a piece of paper

Instructions:

If you roll, for example, 6 and 5, you get one point from the difference between 6 and 5. And you get 11 because 6 + 5 = 11. So your score would be 12.

Or, for another example, if you get 3 and 2, you would get one point from the difference between 3 and 2. And you would get 5 because 3 + 2 = 5. So your score would be 6.

You each roll 8 times by taking turns.

And player 2 rolls first.

And if you get a double such as 1 + 1 you only get two because there is no difference between 1 and 1.

The game is over when each player rolls 8 times.

Use the calculator to add up the score.

FIGURE 6.2.▲ A student-created family math game.

were given the materials and instructions they needed to play the games. I also asked them to make a list of the strategies they used when playing the games at home so we could discuss their thinking when we got together for our next session. I devised the simple form in Figure 6.3 to encourage families to reflect on the insights they gained when doing the games at home.

In general the night felt very successful, although I did make a note to myself to change the openers portion of our next session, two weeks later, when we would focus on another mathematical strand. I wanted to eliminate the large posters that told how to play the games and replace them with individual handouts at each table. I felt this would make the games more accessible.

Family Math suggests a typical program of six to eight sessions, each lasting an hour or two. But there's no need to be typical. I did only two sessions; others have done just one. Appendix A in *Family Math* includes lots of planning suggestions.

Students Take Center Stage

Here's a different way to approach a family math night, taken by my friend Annette Raphel, who had her fourth graders set up a night of estimation activities for their parents. To help the children get ready to create their own activities, Annette first had them rotate through fourteen "estimation centers." Here are descriptions of the centers, along with the clues Annette provided to help get her students thinking:

1. Description: At this station, there were 30 pennies in a translucent film container. Next to the container were the clue card and 10 loose pennies that the children could manipulate.
   Activity: Estimate how many pennies are in the container.
   Clue: Does it help to make a stack of ten pennies?
2. Description: This station contained a balance scale, a pair of giant dice, and 11 cubes. The scale came close to balancing with one die and 9 or 10 cubes, but there were not enough cubes to balance both dice.

Family Math Homework

Names:

We played the game _____
Here are some of our strategies and the mathematical procedures we used to play the games:

FIGURE 6.3.▲ Reporting form for family math homework.

Activity: Estimate how many cubes will balance the dice.

Clue: You can pick up the cubes and the dice in your hands. You can use the scale too!

3. Description: At this station there was a three-minute timer and a stopwatch. The children were not given enough time to wait for all the sand in the timer to empty, but they could time how long it took for a portion of the sand to empty. Not many students were aware that it was probably a three-minute timer; those who were seemed to be interested in seeing whether it was accurate.

   Activity: Estimate how long it will take for the sand in the timer to go down.

   Clue: Does it help to think about how long it will take for half of the sand to go down?

4. Description: The station contained a box about five cubes wide and about ten cubes long. There were twelve cubes for the children to manipulate, enough to lay them across the width of the box or down the length of it, but not enough to do both simultaneously.

   Activity: Estimate how many blocks will cover the bottom of the box.

   Clue: Can you lay out the blocks on the bottom of the box to see how many will go across its width? Can you lay them out to see how many will go down its length?

5. Description: This station contained a bowl of kidney beans, several small identical plastic cups, and several larger identical plastic cups. There were enough beans to fill a small cup about five times, but not enough to fill a large cup, which held about eight times the volume of a small cup.

   Activity: Estimate how many little cups of beans fit into a big cup.

   Clue: Does it help to try to put a few small cups of beans into the large cup?

6. Description: This station had a very thick piece of licorice that was twenty-five inches long. (There was a backup piece of the same length in a plastic bag.)

   Activity: Estimate how long the licorice is.

   Clue: This card is 5 inches wide. Does that help you?

7. Description: At the station were a stack of 125 white cards and a smaller pile of 20 pink cards of the same size and shape.

Activity: Estimate how many white cards are in this stack.

Clue: There are 20 pink cards in the small pile.

8. Description: At this station were an unopened package of Necco Wafers and 10 loose ones. (Crackers or candy that is packed cylindrically would also work fine for this center.)

    Activity: Estimate how many Necco Wafers are in the package.

    Clue: Don't count them. You may use the loose ones to help you.

9. Description: At this station there were a large plastic mixing bowl and two identical glass canning jars (without markings on the side to show capacity). One of the jars had three cups of rice already in it and was sealed. The other jar was empty. A plastic bag held one cup of rice. There was also a funnel, as well as a one-cup measuring cup for verification purposes.

    Activity: Estimate how many cups of rice are in a full jar.

    Clue: There is one cup of rice in this bag. Pour it into the empty jar. Use the bowl so you don't spill anything.

10. Description: At this station was a standard canning jar with 414 lima beans inside. Next to it was a plastic bag containing 100 lima beans.

    Activity: Estimate how many lima beans are in the jar.

    Clue: There are 100 lima beans in the plastic bag.

11. Description: At this station were 15 wooden balls from a baby's game, each weighing about an ounce. There was also a kitchen scale.

    Activity: Estimate how much these balls weigh.

    Clue: Don't take all the balls out. You may weigh one or a few of them.

12. Description: For this station I had outlined a symmetric but intricate shape that would hold 42 tiles. (I folded a piece of one-inch graph paper in half and cut along the lines, unfolded the shape, and traced carefully around it.) There were 15 tiles available to place inside the outline.

    Activity: Estimate the number of tiles it would take to fill this shape.

    Clue: Try putting some of these tiles inside it. Are parts of the shape the same?

13. Activity: Estimate how tall Mrs. Raphel is.

    Clue: Think of how tall you are. Will that help?

14. Description: At this station were a strip of paper 24 inches long and 13 plastic lima beans, each one inch long.

    Activity: Estimate how many lima beans will fit across this paper.

    Clue: Can you figure out how many would fit across half the paper?

The twenty-four students in Annette's class worked in pairs that had been randomly selected. When all the partners had had a chance to experience each of the fourteen centers, Annette brought the group back together again. She discussed both mathematical and social issues with the group: "Getting exact answers is lucky, but getting within a range of the answer shows great skill."

Now these fourth graders were ready to start designing their own centers for family math night. Each child was asked to create an estimation station complete with clue card. Macky's station, for example, featured a bottle of peppercorns. The job was to estimate how many peppercorns were contained in the bottle. His clue card read, "It took me over an hour to count them!"

On family math night, parents were given a clipboard on which to record their estimates, and the kids accompanied them around the room. Parents came up with estimates at each station and when they were all finished, they checked their answers against an oversized answer sheet the children had prepared, to find out whether their estimates were reasonable or unreasonable.

Annette remembers, "The children were very excited to be hosting their parents for the evening and creating math challenges for them. And parents didn't feel as 'on the spot' about their mathematics, since it was more like guessing than doing arithmetic."

The activity Everyday Uses of Mathematics, from *About Teaching Mathematics* (Burns 1992), might work well at the conclusion of an evening focusing on estimation. It makes the point that estimation is an important skill we use every day. In this activity group members are asked to think about how they've used mathematics in the last week or so. Their suggestions (examples include figuring out a tip in a restaurant and determining the amount of fabric needed for curtains) are listed by one person who acts as recorder. The group then indicates whether an exact answer or an estimate is most appropriate in each of the situations. This activity has been done many times, in many different situations, and the group almost always discovers that estimation is most appropriate at least half the time.

Equity Issues

When I asked Marilyn Griego, an associate with the Family Math program, to pass on her suggestions, she reminded me of some important roots of the program. The Family Math parent program, Equals, grew out of an effort to support equity for girls and people of color. When Marilyn conducts Family Math sessions, she emphasizes the important role mathematics has in opening educational and vocational doors for students. She makes a point of telling families that their children will have a much better chance of getting ahead economically if they have solid math skills.

Marilyn also finds ways to involve as many families as possible. She found that the venue in which a program is held can affect who feels comfortable attending. When Marilyn arranged with the neighborhood Boys and Girls Club to have Family Math meetings in their facility, families who had not attended sessions held at the school were enthusiastic participants. That old real estate adage— location, location, location—makes sense in this situation too.

Conclusion

My students' parents nodded their agreement when student teacher Gery Baura said, "If I had been doing problems like this when I was in second grade, I would have had a much better chance of understanding the problems I encountered in the genetics course I had to take for my master's degree." We were in the middle of family math night, and the problem we were doing involved working out all the different ways in which three flavors of ice cream can be arranged on an ice cream cone. Colored cubes were available to represent the three different flavors, and the room was alive with conversation about how to make sure that all the permutations had been found.

Gery's comment helped parents make a connection between the fun they were having and the benefits their children might receive from this kind of an experience. It made me remember the importance of creating opportunities for parents to understand why mathematics reform is so important in our increasingly complex world. Family math nights are an opportunity to do just that, in a fun and relaxed setting.

Conclusion

One day during the course of writing this book, I turned my hair bright red with purplish overtones. I reveal this embarrassment because the experience reminded me that people have a habit of interpreting information in a way that reinforces their own hopes and fears.

The box for the temporary hair dye I used advertised, "Covers 40% gray." I took this statement to mean that if I used the product, about half of the gray hair on my head would take on the dye color, leaving me with some streaks of gray in a nicely highlighted head of auburn hair. I liked this idea, because I secretly hoped no one would notice I had succumbed to coloring my hair. I also figured the relatively low percentage meant the dye was so mild it didn't really matter how long I waited before rinsing it off.

I followed the directions for applying the dye and then wrapped my head in plastic before sitting down to work on the manuscript. An hour or so later, I remembered that I needed to rinse. A week and numerous hair washings later I finally got back my natural hair color: plain brown, streaked with a fair amount of gray.

I learned the hard way that "Covers 40% gray" actually means the product will color *all* the gray hair on a head that's less than 50 percent gray *and* that it's really important to leave the dye on for no longer than forty-five minutes—just like the instructions recommend. I chose to interpret fairly straightforward information in a rather convoluted way in order to reassure myself that the product met my needs. I made decisions based on what I wanted to achieve, not on what the product had to offer.

So I'm not surprised when some parents refuse to budge from their own view of what school mathematics should look like, even after I've made an effort to explain why I think that view needs to be broadened. People have a habit of seeing things the way they want to and in a way that is consistent with their own worldview; I'm not going to be able to convince everyone to think the way I do. This attitude saves me from agonizing that I haven't done a good-enough job explaining my position to parents and frees me from taking attacks on my curriculum personally.

As a classroom teacher I'm never able to forget what an enormous job teaching is. So while I was rereading the manuscript of this book one last time, my thoughts turned to how I might feel if someone suggested I try all the ideas incorporated in these pages. My reaction would probably be, *How am I supposed to find time to put so much effort into communicating with parents plus teach my class and fulfill all my other teaching responsibilities? My professional life is taking over my personal life and I don't like it!*

The answer, of course, is to pick and choose among the suggested ideas based on your own situation, finding ways to build on what you are already doing. Even I don't do all these things every year for every student. I do the best I can and then work at giving up the guilt I feel when I don't get a newsletter out as often as I would like or when I send home a homework assignment straight from the teacher's manual.

But I also frequently remind myself that parents are an integral part of my students' lives and that they can be either a positive or a negative force in my professional life. I know that in the long run, taking the time to assure that most parents are working with me will probably take less of my energy than responding piecemeal to negative attitudes about my math curriculum. By being upbeat, informative, and open about my approach to mathematics I'm likely to end up with informed and supportive parents who work for and with my students—and me.

The years have taught me that most parents are eager for their children to have good experiences in school. They welcome the chance to learn about what we're doing in class and come to see that *understanding* the world of mathematics, not just memorizing its rules, provides their children with a brighter future.

Resources for Communicating With Parents About Math

Allison, Linda, and Martha Weston. 1993. *Eenie Meenie Miney Math: Math Play for You and Your Preschooler*. A Brown Paper Preschool book. Boston, MA: Little, Brown.

This book is a collection of games and activities for parents of preschoolers to do as part of their daily lives. It encourages parents to take advantage of learning opportunities wherever they find them. It also suggests activities that parents can structure for their young children with a minimum of preparation. These include creating a puzzle by cutting up the front panel of a cereal box, making patterns with impressions of hands on a smooth stretch of sand, and using a messy room as an opportunity for sorting.

Apelman, Maja, and Julie King. 1993. *Exploring Everyday Math*. Portsmouth, NH: Heinemann.

This excellent source of home/school activities includes many ideas for all elementary grades. Chapter headings under the math activities section include Family History, Supermarket Shopping, Telephone Math, and Cars and Travel. The book has two major themes. One is the notion that math surrounds us every day; the second is that parents know a great deal of math and should be encouraged to engage in mathematical learning and exploration with their children.

Austin, Terri. 1994. *Changing the View: Student-Led Parent Conferences*. Portsmouth, NH: Heinemann.

Austin uses student-led conferences to encourage her sixth graders to take responsibility for their own learning, especially with regard to assessment. In addition to describing how to prepare children to conduct their own conferences with their parents, this book includes many suggestions for ways to link home and school in positive ways throughout the school year.

Burns, Marilyn. 1992. *About Teaching Mathematics: A K–8 Resource*. Sausalito, CA: Math Solutions Publications.

Each of the chapters in part 2, Problem-Solving Activities in the Strands, and part 3, Teaching Arithmetic, includes an introductory overview of one strand of mathematics or one big idea in the strand of number. These overviews can be very useful when communicating with parents. (For instance, under the heading Why Teach Logical Thinking? we read: "The process of reasoning is basic to all mathematics. Mathematics is first and foremost a way of thinking, rather than a body of facts. This is an important distinction for children to understand. At all grade levels, children benefit from experiences that help them gain clarity and precision in their thought processes. This is not only essential for learning mathematics but also has applications in all curriculum subjects and in ordinary life situations.") The language here is straightforward and succinct. Reading these overviews makes me clearer about my teaching goals and also helps me sort through ideas when I'm writing newsletters or preparing presentations to parents.

Burns, Marilyn. 1994. *Mathematics: What Are You Teaching My Child?* 20 min. New York: Scholastic. Videocassette.

Intended primarily for parents, this videotape looks at classrooms that have thinking and reasoning as their major goals. It also explains how teaching mathematics must change in response to the changing demands of the world of work.

Burns, Marilyn. 1998. *Math: Facing an American Phobia.*
Sausalito, CA: Math Solutions Publications.

This book takes a look at the roots of math phobia and suggests
ways this debilitating phenomenon can be avoided. It encourages
us to see math as a friendly part of our world and to teach in ways
that draw on kids' natural interest and ability to learn mathematics. It's a great read for parents and teachers.

California State Department of Education. 1987. *Mathematics
Model Curriculum Guide: Kindergarten Through Grade Eight.*
Sacramento, CA: California State Department of Education.

Kathy Richardson was the principal writer for part 2 of this guide.
Anything that Kathy writes is extremely thoughtful and clear. In
the Essential Understandings section of the book she gets to the
heart of what is significant for many of the strands of mathematics. The short section entitled Teaching for Understanding: Guiding Principles is also very useful when thinking through how
learning takes place. To order, write to Publications Sales, California State Department of Education, P.O. Box 271, Sacramento, CA
95802-0271 or call (916) 445-1260.

Corwin, Rebecca B. 1996. *Talking Mathematics: Supporting
Children's Voices.* Portsmouth, NH: Heinemann. Book and
videocassette.

The book focuses on the role of discourse in the mathematics
program and makes a strong argument for experiential learning
that includes lots of mathematical talk. It suggests many reasons
to put aside a mathematics program that relies on rote memorization and replace it with one that encourages children to develop
"a curious, problem-solving habit of mind." The introductory
video of the same name shows clips of children doing mathematics and talking about their mathematical reasoning.

Developmental Studies Center. 1995. *Number Power: A
Cooperative Approach to Mathematics and Social Development.*
K–6 Series. Reading, MA: Addison-Wesley.

The unit overviews in this series include notes about number understanding, as well as suggested parent letters to send home. As the subtitle suggests, it also offers suggestions for making cooperative group work successful. The sections on social development can be useful when talking to parents about the importance of preparing students to work together effectively while solving problems.

Kaye, Peggy. 1987. *Games for Math: Playful Ways to Help Your Child Learn Math from Kindergarten to Third Grade*. New York: Pantheon.

The general introduction and the beginning of each chapter provide clear explanations, written for parents, about how children learn. Examples of how real children approach problems and how their approaches relate to mathematical development make this book a great model for written communication with parents. It also has ideas you can pass along to parents for helping their children with specific math concepts.

Math Solutions Publications. Math By All Means Series. Sausalito, CA: Math Solutions Publications.

This series includes various titles by various authors on a variety of math topics for the elementary grades. In addition to including suggestions for parent letters, the more recently published books often have a section, entitled Goals for Instruction, that lists the big mathematical ideas that will be encountered by students during the unit. Spending time pondering these ideas better prepares me to teach the unit. It also helps me help parents understand the choices that I've made for my mathematics program.

Mokros, Jan. 1996. *Beyond Facts and Flashcards: Exploring Math with Your Kids*. Portsmouth, NH: Heinemann.

This is a great resource to recommend to parents. It was written to help parents help their children with math and includes a description of math literacy that is helpful to teachers and parents alike. The mathematical activities are described under such topics as Coupon Math, Traveling Math, Sick-in-Bed Math, to name just a few. Each section includes ideas for kids in grades K–6.

Richardson, Kathy. 1984. *Developing Number Concepts Using Unifix Cubes*. Reading, MA: Addison-Wesley.

Each chapter in this book begins with a section entitled What You Need to Know About . . . (Beginning Number Concepts, Beginning Addition and Subtraction, Place Value, etc.). If primary teachers made these explanations available to parents, we'd have a parent community that was well informed about how mathematical development takes place in young children. Kathy's writing is both simple and profound.

Richardson, Kathy. 1990. *A Look at Children's Thinking*. Norman, OK: Educational Enrichment. Videocassettes.

These videos offer kindergarten and first- and second-grade teachers ideas for individual number assessments to use in curriculum planning and for parent conferences. They offer insights into how young children think about important number concepts and suggest ways to question young children about their thinking. For ordering information, call (405) 321-3275.

Stenmark, Jean Kerr, Virginia Thompson, and Ruth Cossey. 1986. *Family Math*. Coates, Grace Dávila, and Jean Kerr Stenmark. 1997. *Family Math for Young Children*. Berkeley, CA: Regents, University of California.

In addition to offering many mathematical activities that can be used during a family math session, these books also provide a blueprint for organizing a family math program for students and parents. Family Math, an outgrowth of Equals, offers workshops throughout the country for teachers and other interested individuals. For more information about Equals books, call (510) 642-1910; for information about workshops and programs call (510) 642-1823.

TERC. 1995. *Investigations in Number, Data, and Space*. K–6
Series. Palo Alto, CA: Dale Seymour.

The teacher notes interspersed throughout each book in this series are invaluable sources of information and language for the
classroom teacher. The series aims not only to provide an excellent curriculum for students but also to give the classroom
teacher a deeper understanding of the teaching/learning process.
I draw heavily from this series when thinking through what I
want to say to children and parents. The series also features dialogue boxes that describe the interaction among children and
teachers during mathematics lessons and that can be used as a
model for how to describe one's own classroom to parents. The
blackline masters section of each volume in the series includes a
family letter.